Good Words for THE CONSCIOUS COMMUNICATOR: THE FINE ART OF NOT SAYING STUPID SH*T

"This is the book that's missing from the conversation about equity and inclusivity in the workplace. The need for it is so great that I thought about writing it myself! Thank goodness Janet Stovall and Kim Clark have done the work, based on years of experience and expertise. This book will help a lot of people and a lot of companies."

—**Celeste Headlee** (she/her)
Journalist. Author. Speaker.

"Communications can bring people together or tear them apart, build societies up or burn them down. With so much at stake, we have to move beyond the performative to do the transformative. This book shows us how."

—**Sally Kohn** (she/her)
Author, *The Opposite Of Hate: A Field Guide To Repairing Our Humanity*

"More and more, organizations are being asked to take a stand on issues important to the incoming generation of talent, and they are woefully unprepared—or worse, resistant to using their voice. Stovall and Clark have offered a model that can be utilized to make sure leaders build the organizational muscle of inclusive communications so that they never miss the opportunity to deepen their relationships with key stakeholders in the moments that matter."

—Jennifer Brown (she/her)
Founder of Jennifer Brown Consulting
Author, *Inclusion, How to be an Inclusive Leader*, and *Beyond Diversity*

"There's a thin line between reality and mythology, and communicators have to pick a side. This book will help them pick the right one."

—Dr. Jennifer A. Richeson (she/her)
Philip R. Allen Professor of Psychology, Yale University

"The events of the last few years have brought issues of race, gender, and identity to the forefront of everyday life. Leaders across every industry need to be better equipped to have emotional and difficult conversations in the workplace. Honestly, we can all use help in avoiding saying stupid sh*t. There is no voice I trust more than Janet Stovall to provide clear (and sometimes brutally honest) guidance on how to address these important issues in these intense times."

—David Lee (he/him)
Innovation Leader, TED Speaker

"Communicating clearly under ordinary circumstances is challenging enough in today's world of short attention spans and hyper-divided perspectives. When the subject matter is prickly, the task is even more daunting. Business leaders need more than positive intent, we need DEPTH. This book provides relevant and practical communications guidance with

a business value proposition. It is a must-read for leaders who understand the power of their platform and want to use it for good."

—**Nicole "Nikki" Clifton** (she/her)
President, Social Impact and The UPS Foundation

"*It's not easy writing a book about something that can change the world when there is a system in place today that keeps you from doing that. Seeing these two women step up and speak up to help companies stop saying stupid sh*t is phenomenal. It's needed and urgent, and as a five-time New York Times bestselling author plus now out with my sixth bestseller, I know how important it is to share what you know to improve the world. If you're someone like me who will walk off the planet serving, this is the conversation you need.*

Read this book if you are a leader of a big, middle, or small-sized company, and pay attention to stay in integrity to your core vision and principles and communicate them in depth. Your business revenue and results will thank you for it."

—**Loral Langemeier** (she/her)
Founder of Integrated Wealth Systems

"The Conscious Communicator *by Janet M. Stovall and Kim Clark is a must-read for anyone wanting to enlarge their capacity to engage in our increasingly diverse and complex environment. It invites you into the inquiry of inclusion, and to bring with you not only your skills but your compassion and vulnerability as well. "We find ourselves confronted with the fierce urgency of now," so eloquently prophesied by Rev. Dr. Martin Luther King, Jr. There is not a minute to waste in becoming more civil, collaborative, and celebratory.*"

—**Rev. Deborah L. Johnson** (she/her)
Author, *The Sacred YES* and *Your Deepest Intent*

"In today's market, workplace culture is as important as title and compensation. Today's job seeker and employee is not simply looking for a job, but a culture that provides meaningful connection. It is critically important that leaders and organizations are intentional with their messaging to nurture this connection. This book provides practical examples to develop authentic messaging that gets to the heart of communication, which is about what is needed and what you want."

—**LaQuenta Jacobs** (she/her)
Chief Diversity Officer
XPO Logistics, Inc.

"The role of PR, Employer Value Proposition agencies, and communications agencies was permanently changed in the summer of 2020. We must rise to the occasion with educated recommendations for our clients. Otherwise, we will be doing them a disservice. We have to gain the skills to go beyond the 'no comment'. This book offers the framework to ask the right questions to put our clients in a position of strength on DEI and social justice messaging."

—**Andy Getsey** (he/him)
Co-founder, Senior Partner
Employera

"I've been fortunate to have a front-row seat as Kim Clark and Janet Stovall have become the nation's top experts in DE&I and social justice communications. I have learned so much from them, and I expect my education is just beginning.

Kim and Janet have been at the forefront of a revolutionary change in corporate communications, as companies have begun to embrace diversity, equity, and inclusion as business imperatives, not just PR positioning.

But that doesn't mean organizations are doing it right—or doing nearly enough. That's why Kim and Janet wrote this book.

At Ragan Consulting, we help companies tell their stories in deep and meaningful ways. In that work, Kim and Janet have wowed our customers with their expertise, compassion, and ability to connect with audiences.

This book is a gift to communicators everywhere, and to those of us who help them get better. Bravo, Kim and Janet!"

—**Jim Ylisela** (he/him)
Co-founder and Senior Consultant
Ragan Consulting Group

"The Conscious Communicator: The fine art of not saying stupid sh*t is the book that all communications professionals need right now. Navigating the world of DEI in your organization is not for the faint of heart.

As internal and external communicators, you are often looked to for what to say and when to say it when it comes to social justice issues. As the conscience of the organization, having a resource like Janet and Kim's book at your fingertips can help provide the confidence to back those decisions up. 10/10 would recommend this to any communicator!"

—**Elizabeth Bunney** (she/her)
Communications Manager
President, International Association of Business Communicators (IABC)
Edmonton Chapter

"Communication professionals and organizations have waited for quite some time for a book like this. The problem is we haven't realized it yet.

The terms Diversity and Inclusion have been safe bets as we tiptoed our way through the last decade or so. And since the trauma of George Floyd's murder, our profession has skated on how to say the obvious to the oblivious. The Conscious Communicator: The fine art of not saying stupid sh*t is your wakeup and clarion call that communications through an equity and social justice lens are achievable.

The Conscious Communicator will teach you how to stay away from the sheltered areas and color outside the lines to get a clear picture of the possibilities. It's more than a road map. It gives permission to look inside yourself and that of your organization and say, DE&I is more than a "special interest."

Stovall and Clark's book faces the challenge of communicating DE&I and social justice issues authentically and consistently. It starts with us, no matter your race, ability, language, or pronouns. This book is something you should carry around for reference and sustenance.

As a Black woman, which will gratefully never change, I have experienced frustration and on a good day, determination. Yes, those good days of determination might just be based on what's inside this book. The more my fellow practitioners read and internalize the nuggets of wisdom here, the more hopeful I will feel.

There are organizations and leaders that we hold up as 'doing a good job with DE&I.' After they read and make Stovall and Clarks' work part of their mission, they will do better."

—Anita Ford Saunders, APR (she/her)
Strategic Communication Consultant
2021–2022 Co-Chair, Diversity and Inclusion Committee
Public Relations Society of America (PRSA)

"This book reminds all of us who are privileged to work in communications that we have the responsibility to unleash the power of words and images as drivers to a more diverse, inclusive and accessible organization. Kim and Janet not only challenge our minds and thoughts, but they give us a methodology to put our work into action. The Conscious Communicator is a ground-breaking book that will help us transform organizations into actors of a most needed social change."

—Imma Folch-Lázaro (she/her)
Worldcom PR Group
EMEA Diversity, Equity and Inclusion Chair

"It can be very rewarding to work in DEI communications for a global company and, at times, completely overwhelming. There's so much to consider, learn and do, and sometimes we just need to take a step back and reflect on the work we're doing, remind ourselves why we're doing it, and think about how we can do it better. This book provides so many opportunities to do just that, it's a must-read for all DEI communicators and has given me even more motivation to keep pushing for more!"

—Gael Adams-Burton (she/her)
Global Diversity, Equity & Inclusion Communications Manager
Siemens, UK

"Communications plays such a critical role in advancing an organization's diversity, equity, and inclusion goals, and it's often hard for communicators to know how to do this. This book offers concrete and practical ways to communicate intentionally and inclusively."

—Kirsten Goodnough (she/her)
Communications Executive in the Canadian Public Service

"If you've been afraid of contracting "open mouth, insert foot" syndrome, your fears are over. In The Conscious Communicator: The Fine Art of Not Saying Stupid Sh*t, Janet Stovall and Kim Clark provide a step-by-step guide to help interrupt our typical knee-jerk reactions and replace them with authentic, meaningful, and effective responses.

Their DEPTH™ Model outlines a methodical approach to help your organization determine if, when, and what to say in response to daily challenges and opportunities. Janet and Kim show that the art of communication can be developed, honed, and mastered. This is a mission-critical skill for everyone responsible for communicating your organization's DEI message."

—April Thomas (she/her)
Chief Solutions Officer, SDMS 360

"San Jose State University received the decision letter to reaccredit San José State after the years-long WSCUC Accreditation Reaffirmation process. But one of the top-level recommendations they made was: "Making the elimination of equity gaps and the promotion of DEI and equitable student outcomes the top priority for the University."

Now, more than ever, it is imperative that we engage with experts like Janet M. Stovall and Kim Clark to create and move our DEI policies forward. I've already pre-ordered the book and will be buying and sharing it with principals in my organization. I'll also be using excerpts in my "Media and Culture" general education course. We are fortunate to already have a relationship with these authors and their book will help us spread the 'good knowledge' wider and farther."

—**Kimb Massey, Ph.D.** (she/her)
Professor of Radio-Television-Film
San Jose State University

"It takes leaders across the business to take responsibility for the language we use and how we communicate in an authentic way when trying to connect to our teams.

We don't always know what to say, and we don't want to say the wrong thing. But we need to say something. We must engage in an ongoing dialogue. Janet and Kim talk about how language leads to behavior in this book and it's advice that all leaders need to hear and act on.

The Conscious Communicator helps executives and leaders better integrate DEI into their communication by providing a solid framework to follow no matter which department or industry you're in. Thank you, Janet and Kim, for including DEI skills for leaders in this much-needed book!"

—**Irana Wasti** (she/her)
Executive, Chief Product Officer

"Before I became a DEI strategist, I crafted political messaging. While some people believe that corporations should stay out of politics because partisanship doesn't belong in the workplace, the reality is that companies influence policy in multiple ways. Customers want to know whether the companies they spend their money with are aligned with their values.

Employees are demanding corporate cultures that protect and embrace them as identity-based political attacks are on the rise. As DEI becomes fundamental to attracting and retaining top talent, and our awareness grows around corporate influence on legislation, companies need to be strategic and consistent about communicating their values.

The Conscious Communicator guides organizations as they navigate the complexity of developing and deploying authentic messaging that builds trust with employees and customers. Companies are well-positioned to create safe, inclusive work environments and have a positive impact on society. This book will help them get there."

—Miriam Khalifa (she/her)
DEI Practitioner

"As an executive leading through challenging times, I found Kim Clark's partnership and guidance invaluable. She helped me connect to my team through communication, land my point, and further my purpose with authenticity and impact.

This book gives other leaders an opportunity to benefit from her insights and approach. Thank you Kim and Janet for making this work inclusive of C-suite leaders who are wanting to drive meaningful progress."

—Lauren Antonoff (she/her)
Tech Executive

"I've been coaching and consulting executives for over 20 years through my businesses. I've seen the power diversity brings to a business because it opens up the business to new ideas and paths through varied experiences and insights. I've also witnessed businesses fail because they became trapped in group thought borne through homogeneity. The 'same' doesn't work anymore in a diversified world.

Leaders must rise up to meet the challenge and opportunity offered through diversity. This book guides you to strengthen your results through diversity and inclusion, as well as social justice issues. Every enlightened organization will answer the wake-up call to advance inclusive diversity not just because it's the right thing to do but because it accelerates our business success."

—**Martha Hanlon** (she/her)
Author, *Rise Up, Leader*
Authentic Marketing, Inc. President
Wide Awake Business, Founder

"It's rare to find a book so wise, yet so accessible. Kim Clark and Janet Stovall challenge us to step up to change with heart, humor, and high hopes for the future of DEI. A must-read for anyone who believes we can have a more inclusive world than the one we have now."

—**Chelsea Delaney** (he/him)
Artist, Writer, and Coach at New Stories Calling

THE FINE ART OF NOT SAYING STUPID SH*T

THE CONSCIOUS COMMUNICATOR

THE FINE ART OF NOT SAYING STUPID SH*T

ADDING DEPTH TO YOUR ORGANIZATION'S COMMUNICATIONS

JANET M. STOVALL AND **KIM CLARK**

PYP **Publish** Your Purpose

For permission requests, write to the publisher, addressed "Attention: Permissions Coordinator," at the address below.

Publish Your Purpose
141 Weston Street, #155
Hartford, CT, 06141

PYP **Publish** Your Purpose

The opinions expressed by the Author are not necessarily those held by Publish Your Purpose.

Ordering Information: Quantity sales and special discounts are available on quantity purchases by corporations, associations, and others. For details, contact the publisher at orders@publishyourpurposepress.com.

Edited by: Nancy Graham-Tillman, Jill Ann Kramek, Chloë Siennah
Cover design by: Bigfish Smallpond Design
Typeset and ebook design by: Amit Dey

Printed in the United States of America.

ISBN: 978-1-955985-97-0 (hardcover)
ISBN: 979-8-88797-150-6 (paperback)
ISBN: 979-8-88797-151-3 (eBook)

Library of Congress Control Number: 2024948534

Second Edition, November 2024

The information contained within this book is strictly for informational purposes. The material may include information, products, or services by third parties. As such, the Author and Publisher do not assume responsibility or liability for any third-party material or opinions. The publisher is not responsible for websites (or their content) that are not owned by the publisher. Readers are advised to do their own due diligence when it comes to making decisions.

Publish Your Purpose is a hybrid publisher of non-fiction books. Our authors are thought leaders, experts in their fields, and visionaries paving the way to social change—from food security to anti-racism. We give underrepresented voices power and a stage to share their stories, speak their truth, and impact their communities. Do you have a book idea you would like us to consider publishing? Please visit PublishYourPurpose.com for more information.

DEDICATED TO

Janet: The word warriors fighting the good fight for truth.

Kim: All those who understand communication seeks connection.

CONTENTS

SECTION 3: THE INFRASTRUCTURE

FOREWORD

BY ANTHONY FOXX

When I was in college, a classmate of mine came out of the closet. This was the early 1990s, we were in the middle of an HIV/AIDS crisis, and there was still a lot of social stigma associated with being LGBTQ+. He was publicly vilified and privately threatened as a result. As a student leader, I felt it was important for me publicly to state my support of him and my opposition to what he was facing on campus. People looked at me oddly, people questioned my judgment, but this was one of those times when I had to take a stand. That moment in my life—one of my earliest memories of being a conscious communicator—has aged well.

I'm constantly trying to understand the connections between my experiences and those of others. It's the only way to bridge the gaps between us. However, just understanding is not enough, and sometimes simply making a statement is not enough.

We're undergoing tremendous demographic shifts, with an increasingly diverse, increasingly influential millennial population. It's a population that listens for and to an organization's statements, looking for and at its actions. They care less about bold promises, aspirational social media posts, and million-dollar pledges. They care about words matching up to actions.

That's why it is really important for companies to figure out not only what to say, but also what to do. Entities with a concrete sense of what they do well and how their core competencies impact issues such as racial justice, can develop tangible and measurable plans. And that calls for communicating—internally and externally—in a conscious way.

Today, an organization's social consciousness can impact the size of its addressable market and can endear or repel customers and employees. Today, companies that historically have avoided controversy recognize that saying nothing can say everything. Now is an uncomfortable time for many companies, which is why my great friend Janet M. Stovall, with her co-author Kim Clark, now bring us a book—*The Conscious Communicator*—that distills their broad experiences in a variety of corporate and non-profit settings to help business leaders understand how to manage these times.

To me, being a conscious communicator means having an awareness of the weight of your silence and the weight of your words. It means leveraging that weight to find the common space between business imperatives and social consciousness. Clearly, not every issue can or needs to be addressed by every entity or business leader. The art is knowing when and how best to speak up. When are we best positioned to make an impact in a firestorm of unrest? When does our unique voice carry particular weight? How do we motivate our employees to join us in taking decisive action? What burdens and opportunities come with leading versus following the crowd on controversial issues?

The Conscious Communicator will help leaders understand how to manage through this incredibly complicated environment, to lead with authority, clarity, and integrity. That's what the 21st century demands.

Anthony Foxx

National political leader

INTRODUCTION

Language is very powerful.
Language does not just describe reality.
Language creates the reality it describes.

—Bishop Desmond Tutu, South African Anglican
bishop and human rights activist

A CEO sends a text blaming parents for failing their kids, then it shows up on social media. Employees stage walkouts at major companies protesting their leaders' silence on key issues that directly impact them. A clothing store has white models wearing shirts saying, "I'm Blackity Black" as part of their Black History Month attire. A major brand trademarks Juneteenth and sells ice cream under the name with no benefit for the Black community, financial or otherwise, and minimizes the significance of the holiday. After the murder of George Floyd, more than 950 brands began posting black squares via social media.[1] Intended to be symbols of online activism, most of these posts came with empty statements of solidarity and commitments where few followed through.

HOW WE ARRIVED IN THIS MOMENT

Decades in the making, a global racial reckoning launched a great awakening that gave power and voice back to the people. Brands always want to be seen as the good guys, even when their business practices create and/or reinforce systemic issues and oppression. We are moving forward now. We are shifting from having unconscious bias determine our communications to becoming conscious communicators.

To be fair, organizations haven't been pressured to take a stance on social justice situations and diversity, equity, and inclusion (DEI) issues until recently. Some companies have been more proactive for years, but the vast majority haven't, making them out of touch when they try to respond. Even the companies that have been proactive still struggle with having the right hand know what the left hand is doing and ending up in hot water when business practices are counterproductive to messaging.

Once upon a time, DEI was a Human Resources (HR) issue and social justice was one of those things—like politics and religion—that didn't belong in the workplace. Corporate communications thought DEI didn't pertain to them and that social justice wasn't polite conversation for the office. Then, in 2020, the sh*t hit the fan.

The year started with the outbreak of COVID-19, the global pandemic that claimed the lives of millions and put healthcare disparity center stage. By May, Ahmaud Arbery had been murdered for jogging while Black; Breonna Taylor for sleeping while Black, and George Floyd

---

[1] Dumenco, Simon. "More Than 950 Brands Participated In 'blackout Tuesday' On Instagram, Plus The Latest Jobs Numbers In Context: Datacenter Weekly." AdAge. n.d. https://adage.com/article/datacenter/more-950-brands-participated-blackout-tuesday-instagram-plus-latest-jobs-numbers-context-datacenter/2260916.

for trying to breathe while Black—shining a light on systemic racism, racial inequality, and the need for police reform. Droughts and floods, wildfires, and hurricanes made climate change real.

Employee vocalization grew as social media exploded with marches and protests on a wide array of social issues. COVID-19 work-from-home blurred the lines between the home and office for desk and knowledge workers; employees got real about what truly mattered in life and a lot more demanding of their organizations to do likewise.

Suddenly, communicators were called upon to make significant messaging decisions on behalf of companies and leaders and put change-focused communication skills to work. We always knew our value; it took a global pandemic and global social upheaval for organizations to figure it out, too.

And now, we find ourselves in new territory. We've longed to shift from old-school order takers and organizational note writers to strategic advisors and consultants with fingers on the employee pulse. Here's our chance. But we cannot be effective without building our DEI and social justice communications skills. This is the new normal, and how communications will be done moving forward.

WHY WE WROTE THIS BOOK

A communicator, as defined in this book, is a professional content creator who speaks on behalf of organizations; messaging internally and externally through leaders or channels, regardless of "communications" being formally in their title. There are smaller companies with and without formal communicators who hire agencies, contractors, marketers, or HR consultants. If these folks are not skilled and conscious in their communications, they are likely to cause unintentional harm and make misguided recommendations. The guidance from agencies to "say nothing" is not enough and shows a lack of preparation for their clients. This book offers guidance for having the conversations, building the infrastructure, and making the investments and decisions necessary for organizations to communicate from a position of strength on DEI and social justice-related issues.

We wrote this book to help us, as a community and movement of conscious communicators, build our DEI and social justice communication skills, see our work through a DEI LENS, and learn how to give our content depth so we aren't complicit in performative communications. We want to clearly validate what communicators are feeling about some of the communications we've had to deliver: knowing something wasn't right, people were missing from the process, or what we were saying wasn't true. Perhaps we didn't know what was off or how to fix it or what to do. We'll cover that. Actually, this book as a whole is a way to CYA (cover your ass). We've been through it, we've sat in your seat, we know what it's like and how it eats us up inside when we feel stuck or even gross about the work we're putting out. We need to remember that we have options; we need to get out of the corners we've painted ourselves into and free ourselves to take leaders and companies into the healing direction of history in order to have a future.

The book is organized into three sections: The Context, The Model, and The Infrastructure. We need to understand where we are and how we got here to understand the need and urgency for a framework that directs our introspective discussions, adds depth to our communications, and builds behind-the-scenes skills and infrastructure that set us up for success.

We will introduce DEI and social justice communication skill sets, inclusive language, and visual representation, and we will explain why they are critical to a communicator's role from now on. At the end of the book, you'll find a list of definitions to establish a shared language. We'll talk about hesitant leaders, fractured stakeholders, needed infrastructure, budgeting, and how to navigate difference dialogues to gain the traction we need to be heard and recognized for the value we bring. We've brought in communications thought leaders, and leaders who engage them, to share their insights and demonstrate the value of varying experiences to produce a greater outcome.

And, the pièce de résistance: introducing The DEPTH Model™. The DEPTH Model encapsulates five areas that deserve introspection and implementation to go beyond the surface-y, virtue-signaling kinds of communications we've been creating. The DEPTH Model is an objective approach to handling subjective topics. As we wade into the waters of social justice issues and DEI content, many of us feel squishy, uneasy, torn. This model of five pillars gives us a framework that empowers us to be more grounded, focus on desired outcomes, and communicate from a position of strength and objectivity.

WHO THIS BOOK IS FOR

Communication teams reading this book can be broken into three audiences, based on audience segmentation, categorized by author and business consultant, Martha Hanlon:[2]

- ▸ *Preactive* teams are poking around, dabbling in knowledge by reading some articles here and there, but not doing anything.

- ▸ *Proactive* communicators pay attention to what's going on socially in the country and world, and culturally inside the company. The team recognizes things are changing and they need to do something about it in the organization. They may have listening sessions, acknowledge Pride month in the company newsletter with a rainbow company logo, or convince the company to make Juneteenth and Martin Luther King Jr. Day company holidays. They feel so good about all of

---

[2] Hanlon, Martha. n.d. https://www.wideawakebusiness.com.

that, that they may feel like there's no longer a problem at the company now. Everything's good! (Uh, no.)

- ▸ *Reactive* communicator teams have been busted by employees and/or customers for something they've said or done (or what they've *not* said or done). They don't have a foundation to stand on and end up digging deeper holes. They also feel vulnerable to criticism and fear the consequences of what other companies have experienced.

Every organization on this spectrum needs this guide. We hear you. We get you. We feel you. This book is for you. Welcome. Glad you're here.

SECTION 1
THE CONTEXT

*The vision of our DEI work must be greater
than the pain that makes it necessary.*

CHAPTER 1

THE COMMUNICATOR'S CONTEXT

*Words are things, I'm convinced. You must be careful about the
words you use or the words you allow to be used in your house.
You must be careful about calling people out of their names
using racial pejoratives and sexual pejoratives and all that
ignorance. Don't do that. Someday we'll be able to measure the
power of words. I think they are things. I think they get on the
walls, they get in your wallpaper, they get in your rugs, in your
upholstery, in your clothes and finally into you.*

—Dr. Maya Angelou, Pulitzer Prize winner, poet

Let's be real. We're trying to do something that's never been done before: create a diverse, equitable, and inclusive workplace. It's never existed in a capitalistic society and yet here we are, in the roles we have, in this time in history, at a time such as this. Many of us are in environments that were never designed for us. We've shown up, realized what's going on, and now it's time for education, awareness, and action

3

for workplace communications to be designed with the historically marginalized in mind.

THE SOCIAL AGREEMENT

Before we get started, we need a social agreement to establish that this is a place of learning and that changing how we do our work is expected to have bumps in the road. Most people love to learn, but hate to change; we must remember this for ourselves and when working with leaders, employees, and stakeholders.

Social agreements help set expectations, mitigate undermining, and welcome everyone to the conversation. We recommend using social agreements to start meetings and training sessions as one way to demonstrate inclusion. Here's an example:

- ▸ What we're trying to do has never been done before. We're figuring it out together.

- ▸ Give permission to be imperfect. Offer each other grace.

- ▸ Stay open. Learning is just on the other side.

- ▸ Bear the discomfort of progress to create safe spaces.

- ▸ Keep opting in, even when it gets difficult. Stick with it. People are worth it.

- ▸ Practice respectful speech.

We're working towards the change we want to see in the world. And with learning (and unlearning), it's not a matter of *if* we make mistakes, but when—because we *will* make mistakes. So, we need to give each other some grace, since we're all on different paths and levels of awareness. Notice we didn't say "right" and "wrong." This work isn't about judgment, but conscious awareness of our role, our place, and our power in the world.

THE ROLE OF COMMUNICATORS IN DEI

We're just going to dive right in. Traditional public relations, internal communications, and executive communications exist to reinforce the status quo. For example, fundamental internal communication is crafted through the framework of what we want employees to 1) know, 2) feel, and 3) do. Traditionally, that means force-fitting messaging, restricting what people know to control what we want them to feel, and limiting what they can do. Becoming conscious communicators by applying a DEI LENS to our work means expanding the topics, options, and actions our audience can experience—making room. We'll be better informed and prepared, co-creating the employee experience, delivering more productive outcomes, and building or repairing trust with these skills.

A host of acronyms describe this space: DEI (diversity, equity, inclusion), DIB (diversity, inclusion, belonging), I&D (inclusion and diversity), and JEDI (justice, equity, diversity, inclusion). One of the newest, IDEA (inclusion, diversity, equity, accessibility)—or DEIA in the public sector—recognizes the 15% of the world's population, or an estimated one billion people, living with disabilities.[3] Each is a customized statement about where work is focused and what's prioritized at each organization.

For communicators, diversity is, for example, establishing a representative, balanced team with various lived and professional experiences, as well as building relationships internally and externally to establish a strong network for inclusive insight. This leads to more diverse representation in our work, more intentionality in inclusive language, and visual inclusion in our content.

---

[3] "Factsheet on Persons with Disabilities." The United Nations. Accessed January 11, 2022. https://www.un.org/development/desa/disabilities/resources/factsheet-on-persons-with-disabilities.html.

Equity for communications could mean, for example, a review of communication channels, tools, and systems to ensure accessibility, such as captions and universal design features, as well as access to information for non-desk employees. It calls for partnering with brand and IT teams to build pronouns, audio recordings, and name pronunciations into our tools and email signatures to help our colleagues address us with correct pronouns and say our names accurately and respectfully. Another form of equity is reducing barriers for employees to reach out to us, share their stories, and give us feedback.

Inclusion is a verb, an action; something we do intentionally. Inclusion within the communications team looks like having the needed voices and experiences in the room from the beginning of a project and heeding what they say throughout the process. Inclusion is depth in storytelling through every day and month of the year, not just heritage months and awareness days. We tell stories as they are told by those who lived them, including the rawness and authenticity of the experience. We understand the difference between cultural appropriation and cultural appreciation. We stop editing stories with corporate messages and jargon and centering the company as the hero. Any good story has obstacles and learning opportunities. The people in our stories are the ones to center. Our stories should change behavior and call people to action. Let's not tell stories in vain. Retelling stories can be traumatic for some employees. First, we must emotionally connect readers by including stories we've never heard before by people we haven't heard from before.

People make up a company and people make up our customers. Our organizations have a role and responsibility in society, simply because we are global citizens and members of the human race. Many (all?) of the inequities in society stem from economically-driven business decisions. Companies put their social stances where their money is, spending on issues and legislation that benefit their bottom lines. Seldom are these positions articulated. Rather, they are passed off as "how business gets done." As we intentionally narrow the distance between what leaders say and what an organization does (the say/do gap), conscious communication becomes how business gets done. Centuries of decisions have brought us to a movement (not moment) of reckoning across the -isms: classism, heterosexism, ethnocentrism, religious oppression, ableism, racism, sexism/genderism, ageism, and more.

We believe communicators can and should lead DEI work in organizations. We can role model inclusivity, respect, and accessibility. We must start from where we are, do what is before us to do, work with what we have, and push for more. And our work begins with language.

IT'S ALL ABOUT LANGUAGE

Resistance to cultivating new sensitivities often emerges around the usage of language. Language creates images as it conveys information. Descriptions and phrases become portraits that shape our thinking. Language affects our perceptions of others, defines our relationship to them, and creates the context for our analysis of inclusion. And, as Alok Vaid-Menon says, "This is actually the purpose of language—to give meaning to concepts as they evolve."[4]

Rev. Deborah L. Johnson, in her 40+ years of diversity consulting, has coined the idea of "majority coding" in company communications and language. She says the more marginalized one's position in society, the more aware they are of the nuances of power and privilege, which are most often culturally "coded."[5] When one is in the majority position, the code is in their own language. There is no need for introspection or exploration; it is understood and is the norm. Speakers are rarely cognizant or appreciative of the difficulty for someone else to learn the language. Organizations have their own language, usually with coding of the majority culture.

---

[4] Vaid-Menon, Alok. *Beyond the Gender Binary*. Penguin Workshop, 2020.

[5] "Reverend Deborah L. Johnson." Deborah L. Johnson. https://deborahljohnson.org.

Language also drives accountability. Communicators are very good at holding people accountable for what they say, for what they promise by bridging the say/do gap. We help communicate the brand promise. We're the ones who must prove that our companies are living up to it. We can't do that if the stuff isn't there. What if companies allowed communicators to double down on DEI issues with the same energy they require them to double down on product and service promises? The gaps would narrow and communications people could argue from positions of expertise and experience.

According to Johnson, a company's language, the manner in which it articulates what it is doing, enables employees to anticipate and prepare for what lies ahead—for better or for worse.

The language that a company uses reflects:

► its intent,

► how conscious or unconscious it is about diversity issues,

► how likely its employees are to encounter certain experiences,

► the degree to which employees are seen and valued,

► how safe it is to take risks,

► the level of authenticity employees will have to trade in to progress there,

► how much effort it is making to ensure employee success, and

► how accountable it is willing to hold itself and its employees for implementation and infringements.

We can't afford to operate on fuzzy logic or be unintentional and unthoughtful. We have a responsibility to be smart and intentional about what we're doing. It's not only a responsibility, it's also an opportunity.

DEI COMMUNICATION STARTS WITH WHY

Simon Sinek is famous for his TED Talk, "How Great Leaders Inspire Action," better known as "Start with Why," which later became a book. He codifies the key differentiator that makes companies great: They know their why, their how, and their what. Most companies know their *what*, some know their *how*, but few know their *why*.

Sinek says, "The inspired leaders and the inspired organizations—regardless of their size or their industry—all think, act, and communicate from the inside out."[6] When we don't, when we are like everyone else and try to portray an outside that's not true to the inside, no matter how often we replace the siding of our house, it's still rotting underneath and will, in time, show its ugliness and the facade will fall.

Harvard Business Review published an article called, "Survey: What Diversity and Inclusion Policies Do Employees Actually Want?" based on research conducted by Boston Consulting Group, which included 16,000 employees from companies in 14 countries. A total of 96–98% of companies with a 1,000 or more employees that have DEI programs reported that 75% of underrepresented groups do not feel *any* personal benefit.[7]

What this tells us is that most companies don't know why they are doing DEI, at least not beyond a compliance mandate. The discussions and decisions around what DEI work means, what to prioritize, fund, resource, and measure often do not include those who will benefit most from the work. This is why most DEI efforts fail. But for communicators, such failure can be an opportunity.

---

[6] Sinek, Simon. n.d. https://simonsinek.com.

[7] "Survey: What Diversity and Inclusion Policies Do Employees Actually Want?" Harvard Business Review.

We are very good at cutting through the BS and shining the light in dark places. That's what we do as communicators. One of the tools we have in our belts is to do what Sinek says and simply ask, "why?"

> Stakeholder: "We're saying this."
>
> DEI communicator: "Okay, well, why?"
>
> Stakeholder: "Because of this."
>
> DEI communicator: "Okay. Why?"
>
> Stakeholder: "So we can avoid this risk."
>
> DEI communicator: "Okay. Why do we need to avoid that risk? Why can't we deal with it according to our values and aligned with our mission?"

DEI work is not about impressive graphics and videos. It is about making a significant difference in the individual employee's experience and making their day-to-day work life better, safer, and more fulfilling.

No matter how much money organizations spend on splashy photography and external DEI branding, if it's not authentic to the organization and meaningful to the marginalized, then the work becomes a series of one-offs lacking strategy and likely to cause more harm than good.

Too often we are at cross purposes with what we say we want because we don't ground our work in the *why*. Why are we integrating DEI into communications? Not sure? Start with what we believe. We must move beyond "it's the right thing to do," to help organizations speak up on issues happening counter to company values. It's important to employees and customers.

When it comes down to a choice between making payroll or philanthropy, companies—understandably—choose payroll. And that's exactly what we want them to do when payroll means our paycheck. But that's why DEI should never be positioned as philanthropy. There is no universal, enduring standard for what's right, so there's no consistent, sustainable way to anchor business or communications decisions in "the right thing to do." DEI must be communicated as a smart business practice because that's the only way DEI gets embedded in the business, and thus, society.

DEI communications must align the organization's business goals with its business vision, which creates the framework for systems to embed DEI in the actual work of an organization. Simon Sinek puts it succinctly: "The goal is to do business with people [and hire and retain employees] who believe what you believe. If you talk about what you believe, you will attract those who believe what you believe. What you do simply serves as the proof of what you believe."[8]

We have company values to grab and integrate. We have everything we need to answer the questions. We just need to ask them and go through the work to answer them authentically.

KEY TAKEAWAYS

1. Social agreements set expectations, mitigate undermining, and welcome everyone to the conversation.

2. Communicators can and should lead DEI work in organizations by role modeling inclusivity, respect, and accessibility.

3. Language drives accountability; find the why, solve for something, and lead with what you believe.

---

[8] Sinek, Simon. "How Great Leaders Inspire Action." www.ted.com. 2009.

What is Your Deepest Intent?

by Rev. Deborah L. Johnson

We say we want a better world. We say we want equality and inclusion for everyone. We often forget that what we see in the outer world is a reflection of our inner world. We want to have these things, but are we willing to *be* them? Social change is not possible without personal transformation.

Let's not pigeonhole any of the things that we're discussing here into the context of strictly DEI. If we can't do this work at our own individual levels, we're never going to be able to do it in business environments. We're talking about the stuff of life and how we apply it from micro situations to macro situations. Just remember that it's the same stuff of life.

Start with vision. Put your attention on your vision. Human beings tend to pay attention to what is before our eyes, which eclipses our broader vision. When it comes to vision, remember that it is the "why?" of it all that keeps us moving forward. A fundamental framework informing all that I do is: "Pain pushes until vision pulls." Pain can only take you so far. You must have vision to pull you through. The pain of alcoholism may push one into recovery, but the vision of sobriety will be the sustaining factor. The vision of our DEI work must be greater than the pain that makes it necessary.

We develop strategies and reasons for what we're trying to do. Strategies often differ, especially on matters of socio-political consequence. However, if we have a common why, a common reason, such as creating an environment in which everyone can thrive, we can work together despite our differences. Sometimes we have missteps, like saying something that has the complete opposite impact than what was anticipated. But if your why is sincere, your intent pure, everything will turn out all right. There is room for clarification and reconciliation. If this were not so, no relationship could ever survive.

My third book, *Your Deepest Intent*, describes intent as a place of integration. Intent is not a goal, something that you arrive to. Intent happens on the front end, arriving before you do. I cannot emphasize this enough. Your intent arrives before you do. Don't confuse intent with desire, which is mostly longing. The intent is active; happening through us, as us. We, not our plans, are the most important part of its manifestation.

Intent has these three components:

- Alignment – **Where** *are you?* (behavior, thoughts, words, emotions)
- Motivation – **Why** do you want what you want? **Who** do you think you will become?
- Processes – **How** are you going to manifest your intent?

Alignment means bringing it all together. Our thoughts, words, deeds, and feelings must all be moving in the same direction. As human beings, we have a uniquely extraordinary capacity to think one thing, say another, feel something else, yet act entirely different from any of that.

Moving in these different directions puts us at cross-purposes, working against ourselves. Lack of alignment is not neutral; it is counterproductive. It is fruitless to strive for external goals without continuously realigning within.

This same type of alignment must also happen within our companies, for they, too, can be at cross-purposes in the same way. As communicators, it is incumbent upon us to be on the lookout for inconsistencies, not in a judgmental kind of way, but a holistic one. Always have your DEI LENS, an eye out, for where things are not aligning, such as to be at cross-purposes.

Next is motivation. We could spend all day discussing this, because no matter what you say it is, your motivation has an odor, a scent. It has a smell—from a sweet fragrance to a stench. People can smell what is really going on, not only by what you do say, but also by what you don't. You can do something that outwardly appears to be the most generous of gestures. However, if your real motivation behind it is not pure, like to spin or cover up, it will be discerned (if not discovered). No doubt you have experienced this often in your personal life.

As an example, I may be hired to do diversity trainings to supposedly reinforce corporate commitments. However, if I am being brought in as window dressing to merely look good, or to clean up some mess no one knows how to deal with, that motivation cannot be camouflaged. Everybody's going to know it and that motivation is going to undermine any genuine efforts to address DEI issues.

Regarding process: "The consciousness that obtains, sustains." If you want diversity, equity, and inclusion as a result, then you must embody diversity, equity, and inclusion in the process. You can't create an inclusive workplace through judgment and exclusion. You can't have a successful community partnership with unilateral decision-making. At every step along the way, you must be what you want to see when you arrive. Inclusion is doing things *with* people, not just *for* them. If there's something you want to see at the back end, make sure that the processes that you were using embody that.

In matters large and small, people can always tell where you are going simply by observing how you get there—how much you are in alignment, the purity of your motivation, and the coherence of your processes. So, the question to add to your accountability measurements is, "What is our deepest intent?"

Biography

Rev. Dr. Deborah L. Johnson, MBA (she/her) is a dynamic public speaker (including two TEDx Talks), strategist, trainer, and facilitator with over 40 years of professional experience in the field of diversity, equity, and inclusion. Author of The Sacred YES *and* Your Deepest Intent.

CHAPTER 2

THE COMMUNICATOR'S CONSCIOUSNESS

*Companies must bring a business approach to inclusion,
and an inclusive approach to business.*

—The Action to Catalyze Tech (ACT) Report, 2021

As communicators, we've been trained to protect the company by highlighting the good it does, laying low when the not-so-good happens or comes to light, and, of course, being experts at the art of the spin. When we are brought in at the last minute to navigate a change in the company, we're supposed to convince employees it's a great thing. Or post about International Women's Day on Twitter™ with stories of employees saying, "I feel like I belong here!" while a bot runs our company through a database and posts how we pay women significantly less than men.

We weren't ready for this. A college degree might have been a job requirement, but we weren't required to take anthropology, sociology, or psychology classes; excel in women's, Black, Asian, or Hispanic/Latine history; or immerse ourselves in lesbian, gay, bisexual, transgender, and queer+ (LGBTQ+) studies to have the historical and social context for creating communications that address what's going on in society without a lived human experience perspective.

Let's be honest, our communications often are superficial. Spin, lack of transparency, avoidance, out-of-touch corporate messages, highly-edited stories, corporate-speak posts with tons of jargon, good-news-only fluff pieces, and notable silence will not work anymore. Employees and customers require authenticity, transparency, and meaningful action. We must mature as communicators and be the social change agents our organizations need. It isn't easy, and it isn't communication as usual. And some things—like unconscious bias and performative communication—make these things even more difficult.

UNCONSCIOUS BIAS

First in a Zoom meeting, then again in an internal memo, Wells Fargo CEO Charles Scharf blamed his organization's inability to meet DEI goals on availability. In the memo, he wrote, "While it might sound like an excuse, the unfortunate reality is that there is a very limited pool of Black talent to recruit from."[9] Immediate backlash. The next day, Scharf apologized for "making an insensitive comment reflecting my own unconscious bias."[10] The reality, of course, is something different. There's no scarcity of Black talent; the problem is insular professional and social networks and few opportunities for advancement. The original comment was, clearly, stupid sh*t. The apology, however, told the truth.

_____

[9] Moise, I., DiNapoli, J., & Kerber, R. "Exclusive: Wells Fargo CEO ruffles feathers with comments about diverse talent." Reuters. Accessed July 4, 2020. https://www.reuters.com/article/us-global-race-wells-fargo-exclusive/exclusive-wells-fargo-ceo-ruffles-feathers-with-comments-about-diverse-talent-idUSKCN26D2IU.

[10] "Wells Fargo CEO apologizes for remark about diverse talent." Reuters. Accessed July 4, 2022. https://www.reuters.com/article/global-race-wells-fargo/wells-fargo-ceo-apologizes-for-remark-about-diverse-talent-idUSL3N2GK37W.

And Scharf is not alone. Unconscious bias drives our decisions and actions, too.

At its most basic, lizard-brain level, bias is not bad. In fact, it has served humans well, allowing us to evolve by making it possible to process things quickly, with little information. Bias is a mental shortcut that saves energy and capacity in our brains. The problem: humans form societies with other humans and we bring all that bias with us.

Psychologists divide bias into two categories: explicit and implicit. Explicit or conscious bias drives the obvious bad behavior, in which someone is quite clear about their feelings and attitudes, and willing to act on those feelings with intent. Neurologically, explicit bias processes at a conscious level as "declarative, semantic memory, and in words."[11] Explicit bias is spoken and acted bias, ranging from willful exclusion to as overt as physical and verbal harassment.

Implicit or unconscious, bias operates outside of our awareness. The danger of implicit bias is that it can operate in contradiction to what we think we believe and value, automatically seeping into what we decide and do without us really knowing it. For communicators, it's the between-the-lines bias that shapes our content and the unintended exclusion that shapes our teams and networks. It's how "good people" still say harmful sh*t.

Time for the million dollar question: If bias is unconscious, are we responsible for what it makes us do? Yes. Yes, we are. We may not be able to control our initial thoughts, but we *can* control our subsequent actions. Implicit bias is not a get out of stupid sh*t free card.

Making unconscious bias conscious is a process of metacognition, thinking about our thinking. We must examine what and how

---

[11] "Conscious & Unconscious Biases in Health Care: Two types of bias." Georgetown University National Center for Cultural Competence. Accessed July 4, 2022. https://nccc.georgetown.edu/bias/module-3/1.php.

we speak, act, and create—every time, all the time—until examination becomes a habit.

We must ask ourselves questions like, "Why do I believe what I believe?" and, "Why do I say what I say?" and, "What could I say differently?" and, "What about what I'm saying might be exclusive, devaluing someone, and causing harm?" That's hard to do in the beginning, because it's not fun to examine everything, including the things we "know" to be true. But that's the conscious part of conscious communications: putting a conscious layer of thought on our unconscious thoughts and feelings to craft content, build teams, and seek insights with intentional inclusivity. We must make the unconscious, conscious. We must trade the rose-colored glasses for a DEI LENS .

THE DEI LENS

Everything we do and say is influenced by our perspective lenses. DEI communication is no different. When we look at communication through a DEI LENS , we gain perspective on all of our work and interactions (policies, processes, practices, people). Viewing communications through a DEI LENS means thinking and acting beyond ourselves and our own limited experiences. It allows us to learn from others who have different experiences than us. The more we learn, the more we can—proactively—inform the decisions we make and shape the work we do with consideration for others' needs and experiences. The DEI LENS is not something to take on and off; it's a choice to see what we didn't see before, with clarity and focus.

Applying a DEI LENS starts with why. Using the lens to question the "what ifs" and determine why we said or didn't say something in a particular way takes the superficiality out of DEI communications. The lens educates us and allows us to examine other perspectives.

By applying the lens before we speak, we can ask ourselves questions such as:

- "Have I examined this situation in a way that is different from the way I examine other things?"
- "Is it a way that is different from the way I might have examined something that I knew more about or that was closer to me?"
- "Have I asked questions about this?"
- "Have I put on a different lens?"
- "Am I really looking at this differently, or am I just executing?"
- "Am I solely basing my decisions on my own limited experiences and neglecting others' equally valuable different experiences?"

Applying a DEI LENS is definitely learned behavior. It's about being conscious, and it takes practice. We make conscious decisions about the actual words we use. But we are less conscious about the thought or the lack of thought that goes into choosing those words. We don't think about that.

The DEI LENS has many parts, there's no doubt about that. And while we may be careful about how we assemble those pieces, we are less careful and less consistent about which pieces we choose.

It's like a puzzle: we focus on the finished, completed picture. We don't focus on the individual pieces. We don't focus on how they fit together. We don't pay attention to the board on which we assemble them. But all of those elements make up the DEI LENS . Being a conscious communicator means looking at the pieces and the way they fit together; making informed decisions about how we assemble them and paying attention to the surface upon which we put together the big picture. The DEI LENS gives us clarity. The DEI LENS is the difference between performativity and performative language.

WHEN COMMUNICATIONS BECOME PERFORMATIVE

Philosopher John L. Austin described the concept (though he didn't coin the phrase) of performativity, defining performative utterances as statements that are neither true, nor descriptive of action, but rather the actual "doing of an action."[12] As examples, Austin posited that saying "I do" in a marriage ceremony changes one from single to married; "I name this ship the Queen Elizabeth" means the boat has a new identity after the bottle is smashed on its hull; and "I give and bequeath my watch to my brother" at the reading of a will means somebody walks out of it with a new timepiece. Performativity, in other words, is the power of language to create change in the world, to move beyond simply describing to actually being social action. Performative utterances don't just describe a given reality, they change the social reality they describe. Too bad that's not usually how it works for organizations' DEI and social justice statements.

We've seen this play out across organizations, especially since the summer of 2020. Organizations utter messages of "shock" and "solidarity" but fail to take any action. This is performative, and it is the opposite of performativity.

Performative communications demonstrate that the organization hasn't done the work, hasn't built the relationships, hasn't taken introspective time, and hasn't established processes that start, progress, and end with DEI. Performative communications are communications that are unintentional, unsupportable, and unaligned with who we are and what we believe. They are a flashy tap dance to appease or appeal to a disgruntled audience. Performative communications are one-off communications. Companies deliver them and go silent, either because they never intended to advance the issue; underestimated what

---

[12] Austin, J. L., & Urmson, J. O. How to do things with words: The William James lectures delivered at Harvard University in 1955. Harvard Univ. Press. 2009.

it would take to move the needle on it, or were trying to "do the right thing" without doing the smart thing to understand historical or social context.

Performative communications are opportunistic. They seek to leverage a situation for coverage or footage. It's virtue signaling and it often silences voices of protest. Performative communications aren't thoughtful or insightful because there's nothing behind them—no proof, no funding, no accountability, and sometimes not even a promise or commitment. Performative communications are uninformed, not only about history, but also about how they affect others. They offer nothing new, but they sure do feel good to say and hashtag! Like junk food, performative communications taste good in the moment, but they nourish no one and they have unhealthy consequences.

Indeed, performative communications can do tremendous harm to both employees and the brand. When companies make empty statements, employees question their honesty and integrity. And when those employees see external company statements that contradict the internal culture, they call BS. Out loud. On social media. The brand suffers, and customer and community trust lessens. Performative communications sabotage our professional integrity. Communicators cannot be believable, reliable, or viable if we say one thing and do another. Essentially, we are lying. No one likes being lied to.

Performative communication can manifest in four ways: simple, outraged, deflective, and promoted. Each results in superficial exchange, as this graphic depicts.

Four Signs of Performative Communications

What it is	How it looks/sounds	What it offers	What it means	What's true
1. Simple	Few words, clickbait-y image, hashtag du jour	Nothing new	As deep as we go on this	It's always deeper than that
2. Outraged	Angry, disbelieving, nothing new	Surprise at injustice	Privileged to be clueless	It's an everyday thing for those affected
3. Deflective	Blaming, accusatory	Unspecific, undefeatable villain	We're the good guys	It's easy to avoid personal responsibility for systemic problems
4. Promoted	Seeks approval, likes	Ablution, acknowledgement	We did a good thing	It's PERFORMATIVE

For a downloadable copy of this graphic, please visit https://theconsciouscommunicator.com/

When companies promise but don't deliver, it comes back to haunt them. Eventually, the truth always comes out. People will hold companies that made promises in the heat of the social justice moment accountable to deliver on those promises. Employees already are.

KEY TAKEAWAYS

1. Implicit bias is not a get out of stupid sh*t free card.

2. Using a DEI LENS is an acquired skill set and takes ongoing practice and learning. It is fundamental to DEI and social justice communications. Application and change are expected.

3. Credible organizations need to understand what performative communications are and commit to learning what they look like to avoid them.

CHAPTER 3

GETTING IN DEPTH

*He who does not see things in their depth should
not call himself a radical.*

**—Jose Marti, Cuban nationalist, poet,
journalist, translator, professor, and publisher**

C ommenting on social justice or DEI issues can be a tricky endeavor
for a company and its leaders. Do it right and look empathic,
perceptive, and courageous. Do it wrong and risk embarrassment and
looking inept, out of touch, and quite frankly, stupid. Doing DEI and
social justice messaging right calls for communicating with DEPTH.

THE CONSCIOUS BUSINESS

Traditionally, most business leaders didn't wade into the murky waters
of social justice. They weren't expected to respond to racial tensions,
inveigh against inequity, or call out climate change. And they could
shield themselves from 24-hour news cycles related to hard social topics.

But ongoing and escalating social upheaval has lifted the prohibition on talking about things like equity and justice in the workplace. At the same time, a polarized political landscape makes it easier for people to be openly racist, xenophobic, misogynistic, anti-immigrant, and proudly ignorant, all in the name of "my rights." Social media platforms play a critical role in disseminating, amplifying, and even suppressing voices on all sides. Companies suddenly have realized how frightened their employees and customers are. Social upheaval has breached company walls whether we like it or not, and people look to Corporate America for leadership lacking in traditional places like government and religion.

For business leaders, social unrest ushered in entirely new rules of engagement and a whole bunch of new questions. When to speak out? When to stay silent? Jumping into social justice can be risky and it can prompt backlash, especially when performative, knee-jerk communication is used as a social currency without adding any social value. Such stakes beg the question, is social justice truly the responsibility of business and business leaders?

We believe it is. We believe the business world has the best potential to usher in long-overdue change. We believe businesses absolutely should step into social justice matters. And we believe now is exactly the right time to do it.

The 2022 Edelman Trust Barometer surveyed 36,000 respondents in 28 countries to measure who trusts whom and what employees look to as trustworthy sources of information. Once again, employers topped the list as the most trusted source by employees. That said, employees are also wanting more engagement from our businesses on societal issues:

WANT MORE, NOT LESS, BUSINESS ENGAGEMENT ON SOCIETAL ISSUES

Percent who say

On addressing each **societal issue**, business is....

■ not doing enough   □ overstepping

Gap,
*not doing enough
vs. overstepping*

	Climate change	Economic inequality	Workforce reskilling	Access to healthcare	Trustworthy information	Systemic injustice
Gap	43pts	40pts	37pts	34pts	32pts	32pts
not doing enough	52	49	46	42	42	42
overstepping	9	9	9	8	10	10

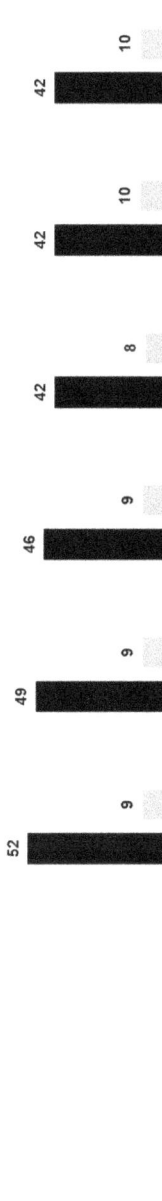

2022 Edelman Trust Barometer. B-S_BND. "Think about business as an institution, and its current level of engagement in addressing societal needs and issues. When it comes to each of the following areas, please indicate if you think business is going too far and overstepping, is doing just the right amount in regard to this authority or is not going far enough in its actions and should be doing more. 9-point scale code 9, That doing enough" code 1). overstepping." General population. 27-mkt avg

Edelman CEO Richard Edelman says, "Government failure has created an over-reliance on businesses to fill the void, a job that private enterprise was not designed to deliver." Respondents want businesses to play a bigger role in climate change, economic inequality, workforce reskilling, and racial injustice: "Every stakeholder group expects business to lean in, with nearly 60% of consumers buying brands based on values, and nearly two-thirds of employees asking companies to take a public stand on issues."[13]

This is a huge opportunity. It's a time when it's hard for people to know what's true, what's misinformation, or intentional disinformation. Even previously well-trusted sources are struggling.

---

[13] *Edelman Report: Cycle of Distrust Threatens Action on Global Challenges.* n.d. World Economic Forum.

MORE CONVINCED WE'RE BEING LIED TO BY SOCIETAL LEADERS

Percent who worry

67%
+8 pts

Journalists and reporters

66%
+9 pts

My country's government leaders

63%
+7 pts

Business leaders

are **purposely trying to mislead people** by saying things they know are false or gross exaggerations

2022 Edelman Trust Barometer. PGR_EMO. Some people worry about many things that others say, may have few concerns. We are interested in what you worry about. Specifically, how much do you worry about each of the following. 9-point scale (top 4 box, worry). Attitudes shown to lan of the sample. General population, 27-mkt avg.

Edelman 15

Employees are looking to leaders and their employers for truth; as communicators, we should fortify the fragile relationship.

With trust in the government and journalism (aka, mainstream media) at an all-time low, companies can energize people, and the voices of business leaders can be clarion calls for empathy, courage, and reason. Inequity is systemic; solving injustice requires systemic solutions. Among all the sectors—public, private, social—the public sector is where a lot of inequity started with unjust laws and discriminatory policies that eventually manifested in the corporate and social sectors. Well, now the public sector is stepping up to fix what it broke with a series of executive orders aimed at advancing Diversity, Equity, Inclusion, and Accessibility (DEIA). That's a great start. Doesn't it make sense for the corporate and social sectors to help?

When business steps in, business can change things. It is the power of the corporate sector, with the money, resources, and abilities that power brings. Companies can make a massive difference for their employees, their customers, and ultimately, society at large—but only if they choose and communicate about the right issues the right way.

Edelman proposes, "Rebuilding trust will require institutions to provide factual information that breaks the cycle of distrust, while leaders must focus on bringing people together on common ground issues—and on long-term thinking and making clear progress on areas of concern."[14]

---

[14] Edelman: https://www.weforum.org/agenda/2022/01/edelman-trust-barometer-2022-report.

RESTORING TRUST
IS KEY TO SOCIETAL STABILITY

Business societal role is here to stay
People want more business leadership, not less.

Demonstrate tangible progress
Restore belief in society's ability to build a better future: show the system works.

Leadership must focus on long-term thinking
Solutions over divisiveness; long-term thinking over short-term gain.

Every institution must provide trustworthy information
Clear, consistent, fact-based information is critical to breaking the cycle of distrust.

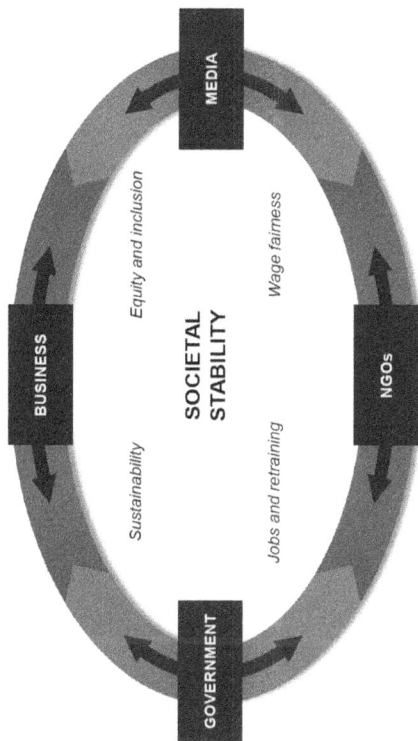

MEDIA

BUSINESS

NGOs

GOVERNMENT

SOCIETAL STABILITY

Equity and inclusion

Wage fairness

Sustainability

Jobs and retraining

Edelman 37

STEP UP OR STEP AWAY

Audiences know authentic messaging when they hear it, and some in particular (looking at you, Gen Z) are relentless in their critiques of corporate response. Corporate communications on social justice issues should be intentional, authentic, and executed only after setting and satisfying strategic criteria for response. That's the right way to step in. The wrong way to step in is by making statements just to avoid being accused of silence (because sometimes silence is golden).

And the bottom line is this: A company will not sustain an issue that is not connected to who they are, what they believe in, or what they do. Companies need not hesitate to engage in social justice causes that fit, causes they can speak to with credibility, and causes they can advance. What companies should avoid is performative communications.

The opposite of performative communications is *transformative* communications: authentic dialogue that actually moves the needle positively on a given issue. Transformative communications require selective consideration, entering a social dialogue, rather than just initiating a corporate monologue, and communicating with depth. Transformative communications bring the power, might, and potential of the business world into the service of changing things. Transformative communications is what The DEPTH Model seeks to operationalize.

THE DEPTH MODEL: THE CONSCIENCE OF CONSCIOUS COMMUNICATIONS

The DEPTH Model allows us to look critically at the things we choose to stand on. It poses a series of questions about what we're going to do, why we're going to do it, and how we will talk about it. It helps us make better commitments because it helps us delineate between what we should or shouldn't be stepping into in the first place.

As communicators, we often *just know* when something is wrong. Maybe we don't know why at the time, but our stupid sh*t-o-meter is always on high alert. Problem is, when the issue has something to do with DEI or social justice, our own bias may hinder our professional intuition. And often, we must justify any hesitancy amid clamoring for a company response, either from a single executive or a mass of employees, whether they are higher or lower on the org chart. An objective model that can be applied consistently provides a specific, repeatable, defensible way to identify fight or flight issues. We can use The DEPTH Model whenever we create communication that in any way tiptoes around or into the DEI or social justice space. It's handy for proactive, strategic communications planning, and for when a crisis occurs.

The model comprises:

- Five key attributes—pillars—of conscious communications;

- Three indicators to determine the appropriateness of the particular message or position; and

- A calculator to rank the advisability of taking action.

The five pillars are depicted in the graphic here, followed by the three indicators:

The DEPTH Model	Definition	Consider (Question)	Clarify (Statement)	Communicate (Actions)
D DELIBERATE	Focused on a specific, articulable problem and solution.	**Define** the problem: What are we solving for?	**Decide** on positioning: "This is what we're saying... and why."	**Do** what matters.
E EDUCATED	Informed by history, current events, diverse perspectives.	**Explore** the history: What do we not know?	**Engage** other views: "I included perspectives from those most affected."	**Expand** the conversation.
P PURPOSEFUL	Aligned with organization's vision and mission.	**Position** the purpose: Is this aligned with the company's mission (and vision)?	**Promote** the purpose: "This is how the message supports our mission, advances our vision."	**Publicize** the purpose.
T TAILORED	Connected to core competencies; aligned with stakeholders and channels.	**Take** stock of capabilities: Is this in our lane?	**Tailor** your message: "We are uniquely positioned to do this."	**Tell** your story.
H HABITUAL	Ongoing; characteristic of the organization's communication efforts; proactive; sustainable.	**Hone** your commitment.	**Hold** the line: "We've said it before and we'll say it again."	**Handle** your business.

For a downloadable copy of this graphic, please visit
https://theconsciouscommunicator.com/

1. Questions to *consider* about whatever position you're taking. It forces you to ask, what is it that you're trying to do with this?

2. Statements to *clarify* whatever position you choose. If you finish the sentence correctly, then you have a stronger sense of where you're going and why.

3. Actions that allow you to *communicate*. Easy-to-remember guidelines that ensure your impact aligns with your intent.

We will explore each concept more in the next section.

KEY TAKEAWAYS

1. Business has the resources, reach, and respect to be a powerful force for positive change in the world.

2. Transformative communication brings the power, might, and potential of the business world into the service of changing things.

3. The DEPTH Model allows us to look critically at the things we choose to stand on.

Calculating DEPTH

At its highest and best use, The DEPTH Model encourages introspection. It slows the communication roll. It encourages you to think about what you're going to say or do. And it serves as a team decision-making tool.

But when time is tight and you must be right, the DEPTH calculator helps you take a stand and support your position. A much shorter analysis, coupled with a scale for measuring the results of that analysis, the DEPTH calculator minimizes the likelihood of saying stupid sh*t when you need to make a quick decision about whether or not to communicate on a sensitive issue. The scale works with the full model, too.

Analyze the Issue

Deliberate: Do we have a clear, articulable goal for stepping out on this?

Educated: Do we know all we need to know about this?

Purposeful: Does this align with our mission and vision?

Tailored: Is this an issue that we can move the needle on—uniquely?

Habitual: Is this something we have talked about before or intend to address going forward?

Calculate DEPTH

- For each attribute, assign a number from 1 to 10 (with 10 being the highest) that represents the strength of response.
- Then average the numbers to get a score.

If the average is 1–4:   Stand down. You risk being performative.

If the average is 5:   Stay still. Unless you can raise the score in one (or more) category, it's not your issue.

If the average is 6–10: Step in. You can communicate with DEPTH.

SECTION 2
THE MODEL

CHAPTER 4
D IS FOR DELIBERATE

Q: What's the biggest myth about writing?
A: That there's any wildness attached to it.
Writing tends to be very deliberate.

—Colm Tóibín, novelist

No company communicates without an ulterior motive. That may sound cynical, but let's face it: corporate communications is about marketing. The problem is it's never *just* about marketing when the subject is DEI or social justice.

WHAT IS DELIBERATE COMMUNICATION?

Being deliberate means being focused on a specific, articulable problem. It can be big or small, but a company should have a good reason for inviting controversy. The best reason is a real problem that the company is best equipped to solve.

Companies need a clear position on why they care and what they're doing about the subject. That position should align with the company's business goals. In the social justice space, the position will likely align with DEI goals as well. The solution offered from that position should bring something different to the problem in some way, either as a function of what you do or who you are.

HOW CONSCIOUS COMMUNICATION IS DELIBERATE

When it comes to DEI or social justice, taking a step means taking a position. So, it's essential to be clear about where your company stands (or wants to stand) on whatever subject it stands for. On some issues, your company may want to position itself as a leader. On any issue, it wants to be positioned favorably. And as communicators operating in performative systems, it's our job to write those positive stories, making sure our leaders and our companies are the good guys—even if they aren't. The solution? Being deliberate.

Deliberate communications are conscious communications because they are attuned, aware, and executed after careful thought about who the company is, what it believes, and what it can do.

WHY DELIBERATE COMMUNICATION IS BENEFICIAL

Being deliberate moves you beyond where you happen to stand based on the timing of an issue and gets you to where you want to stand based on who you are and what you're willing to do. Being deliberate builds credibility, moves the needle, leverages capabilities, and makes it easier for employees to buy in and customers to believe in. Tying what a company stands for to what it exists to do makes it easier for the company to follow through. It encourages executive commitment because it's an extension of what they've already agreed to in some way.

Not being deliberate is thoughtless. Reactionary communication with that approach is how stupid sh*t gets started. Don't do it. Bumbling into a hot topic without having spent time defining your "why" and understanding your (relative) position of authority is a mistake we don't need any more leaders making.

WHAT DELIBERATE COMMUNICATION ISN'T

The opposite of deliberate is accidental, happening by chance, unintentionally, unexpectedly. And have we seen our share of that!

What do accidental communications look like? When intention doesn't line up with impact. Or when a statement not meant for public consumption leaks from an "internal" email or text like the one a CEO of a major fast food chain sent to the mayor of his company's headquarters city. In what he thought was a private text, the CEO blamed the shooting deaths of two children of color—one by police, the other in the company's drive thru—on poor parenting. Newsflash: The Freedom of Information Act makes it possible to find a lot of stupid sh*t. Accidents happen, but some accidents hurt more than others. Missing a financial target is bad, but not insurmountable. Wall Street forgives and forgets as long as numbers trend back upward. Main Street, on the other hand, holds grudges. Missing the mark on a DEI or social justice issue can get you dragged into all forms of media. This kind of communication damages your brand internally and externally and makes people question not just your capability, but your credibility. Avoiding accidents starts with being deliberate communicators.

DELIBERATE COMMUNICATION IN ACTION

Following the murder of George Floyd, Ralph Lauren launched a partnership with Morehouse College and Spelman® College, two Historically Black Colleges and Universities (HBCUs). It is a licensing agreement for traditional HBCU college gear, including varsity jackets.

Ralph Lauren committed to focus on clothes and representation for HBCU students after protests following George Floyd's murder in 2020.

Conceptualized and designed by Morehouse and Spelman alumni at Ralph Lauren, the collection marked several firsts: partnering with a university, developing a campaign with an all-Black cast including its photographer, creative directors, cinematographer, and talent—students, faculty, and alumni at both institutions. The Ralph Lauren Corporate Foundation pledged two million dollars in scholarships for students at Morehouse, Spelman, and 10 other HBCUs.

Ralph Lauren, Executive Chairman and Chief Creative Officer of Ralph Lauren Corporation said, "It's about sharing a more complete and authentic portrait of American style and of the American dream—ensuring stories of Black life and experiences are embedded in the inspiration and aspiration of our brand."[15]

Ralph Lauren's response was DELIBERATE: They focused on a problem, making clear why they cared, and what they were going to do about it.

THE DELIBERATE COMMUNICATOR

Communicators drive organizations to be deliberate in their DEI and social justice communications in three ways: defining problems, deciding on positioning, and doing what matters.

One of our key capabilities as communicators is cutting through the BS to get to the point. This is incredibly valuable when defining the real problem, aka, the issue a company can actually do something about. It's about extracting an actionable problem from the audacious issue. For example, no individual company can solve the audacious issue of

---

[15] "Polo Ralph Lauren Introduces New Collection That Builds Upon Its Historic Partnership With Morehouse and Spelman Colleges." Businesswire.

systemic racism, but by being deliberate, they can develop and deploy actionable efforts aimed at specific aspects of the issue.

Consider UPS®: During the pandemic, UPS® was part of Operation Warp Speed, established "to produce and deliver 300 million doses of safe and effective vaccines … as part of a broader strategy to accelerate the development, manufacturing, and distribution of COVID-19 vaccines, therapeutics, and diagnostics."[16] Though the circumstances were unprecedented, delivering medication was healthcare supply chain business as usual. Being deliberate, however, meant taking a stand on vaccine equity. The result? The UPS® Foundation and UPS® Healthcare joined forces with COVAX, Gavi, The Vaccine Alliance, and CARE to support fast, equitable delivery of COVID-19 vaccines and storage freezers to countries with insufficient access to vaccines, including Asia, South America, and remote regions of Africa.[17] In the U.S., UPS® donated storage freezers to the Navajo Nation to help ensure equitable distribution of the Pfizer vaccine, and worked with other partners to ensure Black communities access to initially scarce supplies of personal protection equipment (PPE).[18,19]

---

[16] Secretary, H. H. S. O. of the, & Assistant Secretary for Public Affairs (ASPA). "Fact Sheet: Explaining Operation Warp Speed." HHS.gov. Accessed February 6, 2022. https://web.archive.org/web/20201219231756/https://www.hhs.gov/coronavirus/explaining-operation-warp-speed/index.html.

[17] "UPS supports equitable distribution of COVID-19 vaccines worldwide." Retrieved from https://about.ups.com/us/en/social-impact/the-ups-foundation/health-humanitarian-relief/ups-supports-equitable-distribution-of-covid-19-vaccines-worldwi.html.

[18] "Delivering what matters: Equitable vaccine access globally." Retrieved from https://about.ups.com/us/en/social-impact/the-ups-foundation/health-humanitarian-relief/delivering-what-matters--equitable-vaccine-access-globally.html.

[19] "Henry Schein Cares Foundation Launches Third Phase of 'Wearing Is Caring' Campaign Public Health Awareness Campaign to Promote Health Equity Regarding COVID-19 Vaccines." Accessed February 5, 2022. https://investor.henryschein.com/news-releases/news-release-details/henry-schein-cares-foundation-launches-third-phase-wearing.

The problem was as unexpected as the pandemic was unprecedented, but UPS® already had a framework for action: a communicator-created model for social justice that situated the company's racial equity work at the intersection of its core capabilities, core values, and core commitment "to help eradicate racial injustice and inequality around the world."[20] This model had been developed several months earlier, in the wake of George Floyd's murder, as a way to guide their racial equity work. When the pandemic hit, UPS® simply had to triangulate capabilities, values, and commitment to arrive at a problem it could actually move the needle on and speak to both authentically and authoritatively. Vaccine inequity was their actionable problem extracted from the audacious issue of systemic inequity.

Deciding on positioning is the second thing communicators do to create deliberate communications. We know how to take a position. It's a function of writing articles, figuring things out, and creating content. We find what we need to support our positions. We investigate what other companies are doing to compare positions. Deliberate communicators are change agents: innovative, inspirational, natural collaborators who are effective at aligning and engaging a myriad of internal and external audiences at all levels. We connect dots, drawing lines from social justice positions to DEI and business goals, then decide on a position from which to tell the powerful stories that emerge.

The third thing communicators do in the name of deliberate communications is help keep leaders honest. We hold them accountable by calling them on themselves. We find dangerous gaps and offer practical bridges. We know the best ways to communicate where, when, and how. That's our value. Exceptional communicators know how to help people sustain their commitments over time through conscious

---

[20] "UPS Calls For Justice And Reform To Advance Equality." Retrieved from https://about.ups.com/us/en/newsroom/press-releases/diversity-equity-inclusion/ups-calls-for-justice-and-reform-to-advance-equality.html.

engagement, and we make our leaders accountable by going back to previous statements to ensure continuity and coherence. We help them do what matters.

Granted, this isn't always easy. Sometimes, the best way to help leaders understand the importance of being deliberate is by showing them what happens when they—or better yet, their peers—are not. To paraphrase Janet's father, "Stupid [sh*t] should hurt." By documenting what isn't deliberate, we see others' best and worst scenarios. We keep it real.

COMMUNICATING WITH DEPTH: BEING DELIBERATE

1. CONSIDER: **Define** the problem.

   Contextualize the problem by finding the actionable problem in the audacious issue.

   Considered question: What are we solving for?

2. CLARIFY: **Decide** on positioning.

   Choose a position by situating the issue at the intersection of the company's core values and core capabilities.

   Clarified statement: This is what ABC company is saying… and why.

3. COMMUNICATE: **Do** what matters.

   Commit to action by triangulating the statement with what you can and will do to solve the problem.

   Committed action: Because ABC company believes X and is uniquely positioned to do Y, we will Z.

KEY TAKEAWAYS

1. Stepping into social justice or communicating about DEI requires taking a position.

2. The best position sits at the intersection of a company's core capabilities, core values, and core commitment.

3. Achieving the optimal position calls for being deliberate: defining the problem, deciding on a position, and doing what matters.

Compassion, Curiosity, Empathy, and Action: Ensuring Our Communications Efforts Respect Vulnerable Audiences

by Shirley Anne Off

I am keenly aware of my privilege in my day-to-day work. As head of communications for Justice Canada, my position as an educated, white, cis-gender woman, a settler on Indigenous lands, and a senior executive in one of the oldest (over 150 years) ministries in government, cannot be ignored.

I also come with my own stories and experiences that inform my worldview. Early in my career, I worked intercultural outreach for a school board in one of Canada's most populous cities. I witnessed the racism that permeates a child's educational experience. I, like everyone else, have deeply personal experiences that shape how we move in the world ... and the decisions we make.

Telling stories motivates me both personally and professionally. As a chief communications officer, it is my job to make sure our work is deliberately inclusive of diverse perspectives and experiences and considers diverse information needs. I am reminded by my own stories and experiences that we must ensure that our efforts are informed by the stories and experiences of our audiences—in particular some of our most vulnerable.

For our communications efforts to resonate, be meaningful and respectful, it is essential that we bring our audiences to the table before we put "pen to paper." Too often, in the rush of our work, communicators focus on the what, not the how or why, and we rely on what we already think we know—and our biases can creep in. But how do we build a practice so that it becomes a muscle we always use?

Effective communications must be multi-faceted. In our case, we need to reach and appeal to media, to legal professionals, and to Canadians.

- ▶ What about reaching and considering the survivor of violence, the victim, their families?

- ▶ What do we do for the woman searching our website for divorce information while her abusive partner is in the next room?

- ▶ How do we recognize the faces behind our criminal justice statistics?

- ▶ How do we support and build trust with the families of the Indigenous women who went missing and never came home or the grandchildren of survivors of residential schools?

- ▶ What type of information does a person with a cognitive disability need when considering medical assistance in dying?

- ▶ How does a visually impaired law student learn about the Criminal Code or the Canadian Charter of Rights and Freedoms?

- ▶ How do transgender men and women want to be portrayed when we talk about banning conversion therapy policies and programs?

It's a lot to consider, but consider it we must. So how do we do this? I lead with intention, curiosity, commitment, and empathy.

Intention and Curiosity: I strive to be an embodied leader. I remain consciously aware of my own experiences and privilege, and I try to measure my own actions against my stated values and the values of the organization. I do not shy away from the idea of conflict or criticism; in fact, I am curious about it. This allows me, with constant work, to bring a trauma-informed, equity, diversity, and inclusion lens to what I do. Most importantly, I try to do this while remaining open to constructive feedback and perpetual learning.

In turn, I work with my management team so that our staff has the training and tools to do this work, to ask the questions, to challenge the historic ways of communicating—to be curious and embodied, so to speak. We must read and learn from the source material that guides our policies. This includes reports from public inquiries and consultations, research studies, and statistics aids.

We need to understand the "why" behind what we do. Without being face-to-face with our audiences, these resources give voice to our audiences. But beyond this, we try—and need to do more—to understand our audience's information needs, their guidance on our communications efforts—and we need to accept the critiques when they come and learn from them.

Commitment: I dedicate the resources so that, whenever possible, we hold consultations and engage with the groups most impacted. These groups include our employee diversity and inclusion advisory committees; engaging with Indigenous Elders, youth, and communities when developing products, visuals, and digital content; listening to what our stakeholders are saying when they champion policies. We need to take their advice, apply it to what we are doing, and learn how to leverage it for future work. It is about building a feedback loop and taking action.

I ask the team to commit to learning from others with this expertise, such as colleagues at the Anti-Racism and Diversity and Inclusion Secretariat, or Accessible Canada and Crown-Indigenous Relations. There is so much shared knowledge to consume and benefit from.

As a management team, we dedicate the financial resources for translation to Indigenous languages, sign language interpretation, plain language, and visually accessible products. We plan to invite Elders to our consultations and press conferences concerning Indigenous policies and programs.

Empathy and Informed Action: I work hard to prioritize listening to others and formed the Diversity and Inclusion Advisory Committee composed of committed staff to guide our team on resources, tools, gaps of understanding, changes to internal practices, and what we must do to improve our efforts to be inclusive. This includes both our function as communicators and the make-up of our teams and management. I try to be authentic and honest so that trust can be built. I recognize the efforts and progress teams and individuals are making. And I ask a lot of questions and try to get things done differently.

Empathy alone is not enough. We also need to act.

These are all examples of what it can look like when communications teams, working together with Indigenous communities, our policy colleagues, and stakeholders, can act deliberately and speak authentically to communities and thereby strengthen relationships. That is what this is all about, really. Relationships.

Go to TheConsciousCommunicator.com to see examples of the projects and work done as a result of this deliberate process.

Biography

Shirley Anne Off (she/her) is a career communicator. For 25 years, she worked for the Canadian federal public service, currently as Head of Communications for Justice Canada. She's worked in the arts, not-for-profit, education, and private sectors. She holds a Masters of Arts in Communications, focusing on feminist cultural policy, from Carleton University and also studied English Literature and Education. She lives and works in Ottawa, Canada, which is on the traditional territory of the Algonquin Anishnaabeg People.

CHAPTER 5

E IS FOR EDUCATED

*Education in the past has been too much
inspiration and too little information.*

—E. Franklin Frazier, sociologist and author

Good hearts and great intentions are hallmarks of the people who
work for DEI and social justice. Organizations, however, need
facts, especially when the issues are DEI and social justice. Subject
matter expertise—and education—are critical.

WHAT IS EDUCATED COMMUNICATION?

Inspired though you may be, as a professional communicator, you
can't tell authentic stories from a position of ignorance. Authenticity
demands facticity (and yes, that is a real word). Being educated means
being informed.

HOW CONSCIOUS COMMUNICATION IS EDUCATED

The very definition of consciousness is knowing something. To be conscious is to be aware. But conscious communication, with its responsibility requirement and liability risk, calls for more than simple awareness. Conscious communication is *educated* communication. Educated communications are conscious because they are informed by history, context, and diverse perspectives.

WHY EDUCATED COMMUNICATION IS BENEFICIAL

Historical research is important, not only for ensuring accuracy, but also for understanding origins. Inequity—the raison d'être for most social justice and all DEI discussions—is systemic. It didn't start yesterday. It was constructed, embedded, and adhered to for so long that it is often invisible to those upholding it.

To communicate accurately about inequity, you must understand its roots. But history is just the starting point. Contemporary context is also important for conscious communication. It's critical to understand what people say on all sides of the issue before taking a position. Doing so may change the stance you choose to take. Even if it doesn't sway your position, at least you won't be caught off guard if what you say falls flat or gets slammed.

Educated communications ensure accuracy and minimize potential blowback. Educated communications create opportunities for bigger debate and enhance the brand. Educated communications make you look smart and credible and help you avoid saying stupid sh*t.

WHAT EDUCATED COMMUNICATION ISN'T

On the issue of racists and racism, Author Ibram X. Kendi is crystal clear: "The opposite of racist isn't 'not racist.' It is anti-racist. There is no in-between safe space of 'not racist.' "[21] So it is, too, with conscious communicators on issues of social justice or DEI: You're either educated or anti-educated. The opposite of educated is not uneducated; it is negligent.

Negligence isn't just sloppy, it's harmful. It perpetuates stereotypes and leaves you open to backlash, which damages credibility and the company's brand. In DEI and social justice communications, there are four niches of negligence one can fall into:

1. **Narrow-minded negligence** is intentional diminishment, blatant prejudice, full on stupid sh*t. Thankfully, it also is uncommon and something most people and companies aren't likely to exhibit. There simply is too much risk and too many checks and balances, including social media. However, it does happen, usually when a high-ranking person—like the CEO—says something without being vetted. This is especially the case now, where social media has eliminated gatekeepers. It's probably the least common niche of negligence because companies and leaders that stay in it don't stay in business long. Entrata founder David Bateman is a prime example. Early one morning, he emailed an anti-Semitic vaccine conspiracy theory to a group, including some of Utah's leading tech CEOs, investors, and other public figures—including its governor. He was gone by that evening.

2. **Negotiable negligence** is overlooking or justifying inequities, usually for the sake of expediency or profit. For example, even though something could affect a group negatively, companies might let it stand because the money to be made or position to be gained is too big to offset the potential loss of righting the wrong. Such moments are rooted

---

[21] Kendi, I. X. *How to be an antiracist*. One World, 2019.

in brand history. Many of the most common brands came—or were brought to—their senses in 2020 and changed the names or packaging. There are still plenty more that didn't.

3. **Negligent negligence** is so common it warrants a redundancy. Negligent negligence is when you omit things, usually because you didn't do your homework. Consider the BBC reporter who interviewed professional tennis player Andy Murray after he won his second straight Olympic gold medal. When the reporter congratulated him for being the first person to earn two gold medals in tennis, Murray replied, "Yeah, NO. Venus and Serena have won four each."[22]

4. **Nonconscious negligence** is the most common and hardest to deal with, because it's rooted in implicit bias, a term coined in 1995 by two psychologists, Mahzarin Banaji and Anthony Greenwald.[23]

[22] Maine, D. A. "Andy Murray politely reminds reporter of the existence of Venus and Serena Williams." ESPN. Accessed June 8, 2022. https://www.espn.com/espnw/culture/the-buzz/story/_/id/17307649/andy-murray-politely-reminds-reporter-existence-venus-serena-williams.

[23] Greenwald, Anthony G., and Mahzarin R. Banaji. "Implicit social cognition: attitudes, self-esteem, and stereotypes." Psychological Review 102.1 (1995): 4.

The Great Re-Branding of 2020

The racial reckoning of 2020 forced several companies to reconsider the names, logos, and packaging of some of America's most iconic brands, which used racist stereotypes of Indigenous and Black people:

The Mammy figure: Aunt Jemima® and Mrs. Butterworth® were both modeled on the mammy figure, traditionally depicted as an overweight, dark-skinned woman wearing a headwrap and shawl. A figure born in the Deep South of Antebellum America and portrayed most famously by Hattie McDaniel in the film *Gone with the Wind*, Mammy was a menial domestic, devoted to the white folks she served, and indeed, often happy in that servitude. The association with such domestic tasks as cooking made mammy a logical choice for branding food, including Aunt Jemima syrup and mixes and Mrs. Butterworth syrup. Kentucky-born Nancy Green, a Civil War-era slave, was the human model for Aunt Jemima.[24] In 2020, PepsiCo® retired Aunt Jemima and rebranded her products as Pearl Milling Company™. Created in 1961 to "evoke the images of a loving grandmother," Mrs. Butterworth's rebranding is under review.[25]

The docile servant: In marketing, Black people "were used extensively during the post-slavery era because they reinforced the stereotype of the docile servant who was always ready to serve humbly," notes Marilyn Kern-Foxworth in her book *Aunt Jemima, Uncle Ben® and Rastus: Blacks in Advertising, Yesterday, Today, and Tomorrow*.[26] In the 1940s, Frank Brown,

[24] "Aunt Jemima Rebrands as Pearl Milling Company." Pepsico.com. Accessed February 7, 2022. https://www.pepsico.com/news/press-release/aunt-jemima-rebrands-as-pearl-milling-company 02092021.

[25] McEvoy, J. "Mrs. Butterworth's to Undergo a 'Complete Brand and Packaging Review' Along with Aunt Jemima, Uncle Ben's." Forbes. Accessed May 9, 2022. https://www.forbes.com/sites/jemimamcevoy/2020/06/17/mrs-butterworths-to-undergo-a-complete-brand-and-packaging-review-along-with-aunt-jemima-uncle-bens.

[26] Kern-Foxworth, M. *Aunt Jemima, Uncle Ben, and Rastus: Blacks in advertising, Yesterday, Today, and Tomorrow*. Greenwood Press, 1994.

head waiter at a Chicago restaurant, posed for the portrait of Uncle Ben, a (possibly) fictitious Black rice farmer from Texas used in packaging. In 2020, MARS Food announced that it would overhaul the branding; in 2021, they did, changing it to Ben's Original™.[27] Michigan chef Frank L. White was the model for the image used on boxes of Cream of Wheat®. White's image actually was an improvement—the product initially featured the fictional character "Rastus," a racist term for simple-minded and irresponsible Black male minstrel-era characters.[28] In September 2020, B&G Foods® announced that it would remove White's image from its packaging.

The Noble (or nonsensical) Savage: Stereotypes of Indigenous peoples typically are oversimplified, inaccurate amalgamations of distinctly different and numerous Indigenous cultures. The term "Eskimo," used by racist, non-Native colonizers who settled in the Arctic is considered derogatory.[29] Acknowledging the offensiveness of its name toward native arctic communities, Dreyer's™ Grand Ice Cream renamed its Eskimo Pie™ ice cream bar to Edy's Pie®.[30] Land O'Lakes® retired Mia, the Indigenous woman who once featured prominently in its iconic logo, from all packaging.[31]

[27] Wallace, A. "Uncle Ben's has a new name: Ben's original." CNN. Accessed February 7, 2022. https://www.cnn.com/2020/09/23/business/uncle-bens-rice-rebrand-bens-original/index.html.

[28] Jones, C. "For faces behind Aunt Jemima, Uncle Ben's and cream of wheat, life transcended stereotype." USA Today. Accessed May 9, 2022. https://www.usatoday.com/story/money/2020/07/10/real-people-behind-aunt-jemima-uncle-ben-cream-of-wheat/3285054001.

[29] Cramer, M. "Maker of Eskimo Pie ice cream will retire 'inappropriate' name." The New York Times. Accessed February 7, 2022. https://www.nytimes.com/2020/06/20/business/dreyers-eskimo-pie-name-change.html.

[30] Valinsky, Jordan. "Eskimo pie is getting rid of its derogatory name." ABC7 Chicago. Accessed May 9, 2022. https://abc7chicago.com/eskimo-pie-new-name-edys-products-brands-that-have-changed-offensive-names-with-racist/6945191/#:~:text=Eskimo%20Pie%20has%20decided%20on,the%20company's%20founders%2C%20Joseph%20Edy.

[31] Wu, K. J. "Land O'Lakes drops the iconic logo of an Indigenous woman from its branding." Smithsonian.com. Accessed February 7, 2022. https://www.smithsonianmag.com/smart-news/mia-land-olakes-iconic-Indigenous-woman-departs-packaging-mixed-reactions-180974760/.

Psychologist and economist Daniel Kahneman offers an even better way to understand what gets in the way of conscious communications. Kahneman divides thinking into two categories: System 1 thinking, which is fast, emotional, and unconscious; and System 2 thinking, which is slower, more logical, and reasoned.[32] System 1 thinking leads to autopilot communications: you get the idea or the story assignment and you write it based on assumptions, your own unconscious beliefs, and maybe what everybody else is saying. You don't slow down to think, because you believe your perceptions are objectively true. They may not be. But operating this way is easy, fast, and efficient.

System 1 thinking is highly efficient. It helps us get the job done and allows us to take advantage of stored knowledge. But we don't control it! Scientists generally agree that 95% of our brain's activity is unconscious. Recent studies using brain scans of unconscious activity in the brain show that we can predict the outcome of a decision seconds before we consciously make that decision.[33] That's not a bad thing most of the time.

However, a key driver of System 1 thinking is unconscious bias, the cognitive shortcuts our brain takes to save energy and make decisions faster. This built-in process is an evolutionary throwback from our hunter-gatherer days when we needed to make fast life-or-death decisions, often with very little information. Again, not a bad thing—most of the time.

The problem with System 1 thinking is that society evolved more than our brains did. The life-and-death decisions our brains were designed to execute aren't really the issue. We have the evolutionary luxury—and professional responsibility—to do better. We are capable

[32] Kahneman, D. *Thinking, fast and slow*. Penguin, 2012.

[33] Haynes, J.D. "Unconscious decisions in the brain." Max-Planck-Gesellschaft. Accessed February 10, 2022. https://www.mpg.de/research/unconscious-decisions-in-the-brain.

of more, and we should dig deeper. When internal inclinations meet external stereotypes, systemic inequities, media, and all the other things that affect our sense of reality, the decisions we think are made consciously may very well be driven by unconscious bias. Decisions like … whose opinion we seek, which stories we tell, how we tell them, and what we choose to research.

The fact is we operate on a continuum between brain-based, biological bias, and bigotry. The bridge between the two is paved with the potential for saying stupid sh*t. The only way to deal with this challenge and stay on the right side of that continuum is with System 2 thinking.

System 2 thinking is at the foundation of conscious communications. It is slow, logical, and dominated by reason. This is the kind of thought grounded in education, thoughtfulness, digging deeper, and seeking to understand. It's not superficial because it's not automatic. You may not be able to control your initial System 1 thought, but with System 2 thinking, you absolutely can manage your subsequent action—which should be asking some follow-up questions and getting educated.

Only one of the four niches of negligence—nonconscious—falls into System 1 thinking. The other three—narrow-minded, negotiable, and negligent—are System 2 thinking. That means they're conscious, which means you can consciously choose not to engage in them. Scientists accept the existence of conscious choice because "we do not know yet where the final decision is made."[34] For conscious communicators, that final decision should be an educated one.

EDUCATED COMMUNICATION IN ACTION

A few years ago, P&G's Tide® detergent and the National Council of La Raza (now UnidosUS) created a campaign for Hispanic Heritage

---

[34] Haynes, J.-D. "Unconscious decisions in the brain." Max-Planck-Gesellschaft. Accessed February 10, 2022. https://www.mpg.de/research/unconscious-decisions-in-the-brain.

Month. In their #WashAwayLabels campaign, people from different ethnic groups, from Cuban to Mexican, offered testimonials on the very real racial slurs, stereotypes, and labels they endure regularly. On white tee shirts, the brand painted racist words like "beaner" and "gangster" in ketchup. Participants then were allowed to wash away the derogatory terms, and create a blank slate.

P&G's and National Council of La Raza's campaign was EDUCATED. They did their homework, finding real people and using real words.

THE EDUCATED COMMUNICATOR

As a communicator, you have two audiences to consider when it comes to education: yourself and everyone else. And you have three areas of erudition or insight to consider: historical, contextual, and factual. Namely, how did we get here?; where are we?; and is this true?

Shakespeare's Polonius said it best: "To thine own self be true."[35] The truth starts with the communicator even if it doesn't end with the communicator. We want to do good work, we value doing a phenomenal job, and we often are our organizations' gatekeepers of knowledge. People look to us for objective truth. They want to trust what we say. The 2022 Edelman Trust Survey suggests they do. We must be educated to make sure they can. That's the responsibility.

But being educated also means we can help shine light in murky places. We can tell authentic stories that challenge long held but decidedly biased beliefs. This is the opportunity.

That's not to say any of this is easy. Sometimes, you get overruled. It's unfortunate, but it happens—frequently. Someone has an opinion that they hold as fact. Maybe another person's bias blocks them from a

---

[35] "Hamlet, Act I, Scene 3, Open Source Shakespeare." Accessed April 24, 2022. https://bit.ly/37zqiGp.

different worldview. What can you do when the people in charge lack knowledge about an issue they want to address? Well, the answer is … it depends on what kind of negligence is at play here.

If it's narrow-minded negligence and the decision-maker has no interest in being educated, polish your resume and start looking elsewhere, unless you really enjoy crisis communications. They will be necessary at some point. There's not much you can do to stop this, but you can ensure you don't exacerbate the issue in response to inevitable blowback.

The same is valid with negotiable negligence. If the sports franchise you're working for insists on using a derogatory term for Indigenous people because they want to sell merch, there is not much a conscious communicator can do except raise the issue. Undoubtedly, someone else already has, to no avail. Fortunately, getting burned on social media is helping many companies rethink their positions.

Negligent negligence is where the communicator can be the hero. Sometimes people don't know what they don't know. One way to make the case to leaders about the critical importance of history, context, and diverse perspectives is by explaining what happens if these things aren't considered. Explain the potential brand damage from being wrong, but also offer the likely brand dividends from being right. Share with them how the issue could expand the brand and give the company a more prominent voice in the space—how the company might lead on this issue. Need to prove your point? Keep a spreadsheet of examples. Track both good and bad, from brands flamed on Twitter™ and CEO missteps, to companies that see their profits rise by being on the customer-approved side of the issue. Speak their language.

But social media can be a friend as well as foe. An excellent place to gather contemporary context is Twitter. Voices that are often unheard in mainstream media have a megaphone on Twitter. A new report by Knight Foundation found that: "Of the news outlets that provide coverage of the topics important to these communities, 71% are perceived as negative."[36]

When you read tweets from communities like Black Twitter, Feminist Twitter, and Asian American Twitter, you get a close-up of their unfiltered perspectives. You get to see what's behind the masks they wear in other spaces and on other platforms. You get to witness them in a space where they feel free to speak their minds. Because, as the same Knight Foundation report found, "Twitter subcultures give voice to issues that mainstream media doesn't cover." Taking the initiative to listen to a diversity of voices on an issue is a conscious decision to be educated. It is reading the room, so to speak, and gives you a defensible justification for not stepping into an issue that doesn't make sense for you to address. But when it comes to contextual literacy, remember: some perspectives outweigh others.

Context education answers the question, "Where are we right now?" Historical education asks, "And how did we get here?" Fortunately, there are lots of resources to help with those two—unless you flat out choose to take a siloed, informational bubble approach to education. The last type of education—facts—seems like the easiest one to conquer, right? But when grown people in influential positions can talk (out loud) about the existence of "alternative facts," we better be a bit more conscientious about what we accept as truth.[37]

Sarah Blakeslee's CRAAP test can help you decide if a website offers facts or echoes stupid sh*t, by asking you to test information for

[36] "How Black Twitter and Other Social Media Communities Interact with Mainstream News." Knightfoundation.org. Accessed June 21, 2022.

[37] "Alternative facts." Wikipedia. Accessed July 2, 2022. https://en.wikipedia.org/wiki/Alternative_facts#:~:text=%22Alternative%20facts%22%20was%20a%20phrase,President%20of%20the%20United%20States.

currency, reliability, authority, and purpose.[38] The Constitutional Rights Foundation suggests being SMART about applying the source, motive, authority, review, and two-sources test.[39]

Being educated is not about being an expert. It's about paying attention, recognizing that your perspective is never *the* perspective, and being intentional about adopting five habits of educated communications:

1. ***Apply the AA___P method.*** The best way to know what matters to the group most affected by whatever the salient issue may be is to ask. A simple rule to remember is, "Ask a [insert most affected here] person," or "AA___P" for short. Examine the lived experience of those living it. For example, if your organization is concerned about voting rights, ask the people whose rights are being curtailed. You don't have to conduct formal focus groups. If you work or socialize with people in the affected group, broach the topic. Initiate a discussion, but be sensitive to the reaction. Sometimes people don't want to talk about difficult issues, even when they're the ones most affected. Maybe they're tired of discussing the topic. Perhaps they feel unsafe discussing it with you or in the situation. Possibly they're just having a bad day. But seeking perspective from those most affected doesn't mean asking them to do the work for you. Do your own research before and after any discussion. Validate what you hear by going online. You can bet Twitter is alive with opinions.

2. ***Assemble an advisory team.*** The safest way to get input is by engaging with people who want to give it. Create a Diversity

---

[38] Blakeslee, Sarah. "The CRAAP Test," LOEX Quarterly: Vol. 31: No. 3, Article 4. https://commons.emich.edu/loexquarterly/vol31/iss3/4.

[39] "Fact finding in the information-age." n.d. Accessed July 2, 2022. https://www.crf-usa.org/images/pdf/fact_finding.pdf.

and Social Justice Advisory Team, a dedicated group of go-to folks who can help you act fast on hot issues. When there's a crisis to address and you're being pushed to get something out there, this proactive approach can help you avoid a frantic scramble for insight and can avert potential fall-out. Just don't assume one person from any group speaks for every group member.

3. *Adopt a shared language.* To mitigate nonconscious negligence, you need a nonthreatening way to identify and talk about unconscious bias. The critical thing to remember about bias is that it's a weak spot, and easier to see in others than in yourself. Be the person who normalizes discussion of bias by identifying it when you see it in your company's content. This may sound tricky, but it isn't. All you have to do is categorize it and then start using those categories to discuss it.

4. *Adjust the approach.* One way to help leaders recognize and avoid their own biases is by making it simple for them. They're busy, and they appreciate simplicity. Vikki Conwell, a strategic communication consultant, employs something she calls "The Grandma Rule:" if she can't explain a point or position to her grandmother, she simplifies and repositions. It's a great rule for working with leaders.

5. *Abbreviate the argument.* When you're trying to help someone else avoid saying stupid sh*t, reduce your argument to three points:

   a. What the issue is, with the historical, contextual, and "human" perspective

   b. Why the company is talking about it

   c. What the company is going to do about it

Sometimes it's better to pose the points as questions and let the other person see how well they do with answering them.

COMMUNICATING WITH DEPTH: GETTING EDUCATED

1. CONSIDER: **Explore** the history.

   Few—we daresay, any—social justice or DEI issues sprang entirely clothed from the forehead of society. Those who fight against the teaching of history are fighting against the sharing of truth. Conscious communication is an ongoing search for truth that requires uncovering, understanding, and incorporating it into everyday business practices. Create conscious communication, and nine times out of 10, nobody will argue with you about it. If they do, then you can be pretty sure there's something else going on. Ask yourself how we got to where we are.

   Considered question: What do we not know about this?

2. CLARIFY: **Engage** other perspectives.

   Get informed insight from diverse sources. Start with the group most affected by the hot topic: people with lived experience, people who have opted-in to bring their personal and/or professional experience to add value to the business, ERGs, etc. Don't just tokenize or grab the nearest marginalized person to review your statements. Talk to as many people from that group as possible to get various opinions and thought processes. Remember, no group is monolithic, so keep that in mind when looking for insight. One perspective isn't *the* perspective. After that, reach out to others who may not be as closely affected but have an opinion—even the opposing one. The bottom line is that when an issue is sensitive, it pays to know as much as you can. This way, you have a wealth of perspectives from which to craft your stories.

Clarified statement: We've sought and included perspectives from those most affected.

3. COMMUNICATE: **Expand** the conversation.

DEI and social justice issues never exist in a vacuum. Never. Look around to see where things stand on all sides of the issue. Context is critical. The increased polarization of opinion and compartmentalization of information means it's a lot easier to find ourselves in information bubbles full of alternative facts. This can be dangerous territory for anyone. It takes vigilance to avoid our own confirmation bias and to see through those obfuscating on both sides. When you come across something within your organization that lacks context, alert someone. It's a delicate dance, for sure, but the idea is to make a habit of examining perspectives. And don't forget to look inside the organization for input. The chief diversity officer or chief human resources officer may be working on something that your communications could benefit from or affect. Consider whose opinion has not been heard.

Communicated action: After careful consideration of A, B, and C, we're doing X.

KEY TAKEAWAYS

1. To communicate accurately about DEI and social justice issues, you must understand both their history and contemporary context.

2. Informed insight from diverse sources—especially those most affected by an issue—is critical.

3. Educated communications create opportunities for bigger debate and enhance the brand.

The Influence of Stereotypes

by *Kimberly Massey, Ph.D.*

> *"Sometimes movies do what governments can't."*
>
> —**Joe Biden**

We Americans spend more time consuming media than doing just about anything else in life. Metrics tell us: "The year of the pandemic could very well be called the year of media consumption. With more time spent at home, more media was inevitably consumed across linear TV, terrestrial radio, and emerging subscription services."[40]

In the simplest of terms, people are in very close and committed relationships with the media and are wildly influenced by them. The World Economic Forum's 2021 report, "Reflecting Society: The State of Diverse Representation in Media and Entertainment," sums it up nicely:

> "The scale of [media] influence is immense. Film production companies, record labels, publishing houses, news outlets, gaming platforms, and sports events command audiences in every corner of the world and every community. Companies in the industry implicitly sign a social contract to contribute to society by informing, educating, and entertaining. Many organizations are realizing that diversity, equity, and inclusion (DE&I) are important for society and for business. In the past six years, corporate diversity roles have more than doubled. Yet few industries can be as impactful in building new narratives

---

[40] Abdow, M. "Media Consumption is Over the Top: How Much and Where to Spend is Key to Maximizing ROI." Forbes. n.d. Retrieved from www.forbes.com.

and enabling social cohesion ... Organizations not only have a social responsibility to represent the consumers of their content, but by doing so, also stand to gain significant financial benefits."[41]

It is undeniable that media affects us all—beyond simply taking up our time. According to the U.S. Bureau of Labor Statistics, there are six times more PR professionals spinning the news than journalists reporting it.[42] And, if you follow the money, "U.S. advertising sales are expected to hit a new all-time high of $259 billion this year ... while global advertising spending is seen hitting a record $657 billion this year."[43]

Beyond advertising and news, programming "stories" are influencing our understandings and perceptions—in frequency and over time—of important issues like racism, stereotypes, prejudices, and explicit/implicit bias. Negative media effects can directly bleed into our everyday lives and lead to destructive behaviors and consequences. And while diversity of media producers, directors, writers, and performers has been shown to reduce objectification and stereotyping as well as to bring forward traditionally media-neglected voices, there remains resistance by corporations to prioritize DEI, even though it has been shown that it is more lucrative to do so.[44]

[41] "Reflecting Society: The State of Diverse Representation in Media and Entertainment." World Economic Forum. n.d.

[42] "National estimates for News Analysts, Reporters, and Journalists." Retrieved from U.S. Bureau of Labor Statistics: https://www.bls.gov/oes/current/oes273023.htm.

[43] Steigrad, A. "Ad Spending Expected to Hit New Highs Post-COVID." Retrieved from New York Post: https://nypost.com/2021/06/14/ad-spending-expected-to-hit-new-highs-post-covid.

[44] Higginbotham, G., Zheng, Z., Yalda, T. (2021). *Beyond Checking a Box: A Lack of Authentically Inclusive Representation Has Costs at the Box Office.* Los Angeles: Center for Scholars and Storytellers, UCLA.

Social scientists and media-effects scholars have spent decades developing, testing, and proving/disproving theories of how media affects our cultures (as groups) and us (as individuals), by seeking to understand how people find and create meaning in their lives through the stories they tell as well as through the stories that are told to them. The effects-study began, (Hypodermic Needle/Bullet Theory) and the focus was more on the sender-message because the (disproved) belief was that audiences were passive and had no control over information that was being "shot" at or into them. Other theories evolved beyond individual messages to find out that long-term, life-long exposure to media messages likely distorts people's worldviews in negative ways (Cultivation Theory). Cultural studies then turned the focus from the message/text to how audiences actively interpret and make meaning from messages. This research indicated that audience members (media consumers) could resist media's intended or preferred meanings and/or come up with their own and socially construct a new reality. This liberty allows for alternative frames of reference to be circulated back into the communication system as well as into the relationship with media.[45]

Knowing all of this: If audiences have power, we need to wield it. Simply talking about the problems of media effects with suggested solutions remains a privileged, ivory-tower rhetorical exercise unless it is followed by action. Education is the best vaccination (so far) against negative media effects. Thankfully, media literacy campaigns and programs have emerged to educate people (especially children) about media effects. And scores of non-profit, media watchdog groups are active.

---

[45] Deuze, M. "McQuail's Media & Mass Communication Theory." Los Angeles: Sage, 2020.

In the end, it isn't enough to hold media producers accountable. It comes down to what we, as individual audience members/ groups do. The public needs to recognize that we have choices, but then follow up by making good ones. If people choose to be passive consumers of media, not questioning the meaning and/ or intent of media makers, all of society must live with the adverse consequences (some more than others). Conversely, if people recognize their power and agency by becoming active audience members and/or producers themselves, we can demand diverse content, strive for as many perspectives as possible, and question and develop our own interpretation of media content based upon our life experience, education, family, and cultural influences.

We can learn that the system doesn't work without us. If we back away from the relationship and demand DEI—especially joined with many others—media will be forced to address our concerns and needs. And, finally, we need to diligently monitor our consumption behaviors: Be skeptical, engage in critical thinking, slow down, check/separate facts from opinion and check the origin, context, or purpose/goal of all information before we share.

Together—and only together—we can socially construct a better reality by making it true every time we engage with media and each other.

Biography

Kimberly Massey, Ph.D. (she/her) is a Professor of Radio-Television-Film (RTVF) at San Jose State University. She is a tireless advocate for media reporting and representation of truth, fairness, and diversity, equity, inclusion. Dr. Massey has written numerous communication conference papers and published several communication articles, books, and book chapters.

CHAPTER 6

P IS FOR PURPOSEFUL

*Service is the rent we pay for being. It is the very purpose
of life, and not something you do in your spare time.*

**—Marian Wright Edelman,
founder of the Children's Defense Fund**

A h, the word purpose. So many meanings from, "You did that on purpose!" to the existential, "What is my purpose in life?" But what does it mean for an organization to be purposeful as it helps right the wrongs of the world? Purposeful companies have a reason to exist beyond just growth and profit. If an organization is in healthcare, for example, it might think its purpose is to help people heal and feel better. However, that's why the industry exists; it's not why that particular organization exists. The company's purpose is its role and impact in society and in the world. It's bigger than just the bottom line.

WHAT IS PURPOSEFUL COMMUNICATION?

A unique purpose motivates employees to show up for something other than a paycheck. And a purpose beyond the company is expected especially by early-in-career generations entering and establishing themselves in the workforce.

In August 2019, The Business Roundtable and 243 chief executive officers signed a modified statement of the purpose of a corporation, committing to move beyond serving shareholders exclusively, to "lead their companies for the benefit of all stakeholders—customers, employees, suppliers, communities, and shareholders."[46]

Customers and employees assumed this was the case already. However, beholden to boards and shareholders, leaders weren't motivated to make the decisions that customers and employees expected. The different priorities and purpose of a company between leaders and employees create the say/do gap that so many communicators deal with daily. We promote the company values, but leaders don't follow them. We talk about the good we're doing in the world in our Corporate Social Responsibility program, while a part of our business is causing environmental harm to Indigenous lands. We release a diversity report and highlight how we're increasing representation in our hiring, and we leave out the percentages of underrepresented groups who left the company during the same time period.

Generally, consumers were (and still are) giving companies the benefit of the doubt. But, even though Edelman says consumers trust companies most, trust is fragile. With more transparency, the emergence of social media, and more people paying closer attention to what organizations are doing and how they do it, if the purpose isn't clear and followed, the marketplace will impose consequences in some form. We can't keep doing what we've been doing, friends. It will not fly.

---

[46] "Business Roundtable Redefines the Purpose of a Corporation to Promote 'an Economy That Serves All Americans.'" Businessroundtable.org.

HOW CONSCIOUS COMMUNICATION
IS PURPOSEFUL

More than anything, purposeful organizations are intentional. Everything they do aligns with their mission and vision, and not just the mission and vision statements used on marketing materials or conference room plaques. Whether it's a service release, a product release, or an explanation of why somebody would want to work there as an employee, the way we message these efforts aligns with our organization's larger purpose. Therefore, these statements of purpose are actionable. They commit us to doing something rather than just saying something. These commitments allow us to get to a place where our intention matches our impact. One part of the company needs to know what other parts of the company are doing so we stay in integrity with the purpose. If one area of the organization is contributing to societal inequities, but we are saying we "stand in solidarity" and pledge a million dollars to an organization desperately working to bring about social equity, that's a key indicator that there's a communication problem across the business. DEI and social justice awareness, action, and communications must be embedded across the organization to help every division be in alignment with the company's purpose. Otherwise, we're sabotaging our own words.

In Chapter One, we talked about Simon Sinek, who asks organizations to be honest about their purpose. To not pretend people are first, not pretend to care about climate impact, and not pretend they are involved in social justice if they aren't. To recognize and admit we've been pretending, we first must truly see our business as interconnected with the communities and culture we serve. We have an impact beyond the products and services we provide, whether we want to or not. Is that impact one of contributing to inequities or reducing harm? We must stay aware of multiple factors to understand our impact in real-time.

WHY PURPOSEFUL COMMUNICATION IS BENEFICIAL

Purposeful communication keeps us from doing the work outside the walls in a foundationless way. In other words, it keeps us from saying and doing stupid sh*t. However, it also brings people into our companies in a way that can enrich the work inside the walls. For many, matching one's personal purpose to a company's purpose is the ideal job. And that's when it goes from a job to a career; where we have increased productivity and off-the-charts engagement. When an employee's values align with company values and both parties are living up to those values, the potential for fulfillment and motivation is limitless.

Purposeful communication is one more thing that builds trust and reputation. Think of a scene in a TV show or a movie, or even a cartoon where someone in the desert runs towards a heat mirage. Picture the elation they feel as they get closer to the beautiful thing in front of them. Then picture the collapse and confusion on their faces as they realize it wasn't real and they've fallen for an illusion. Companies who do this to people inflict harm: the bait and switch, the promise unfulfilled, the dream deferred, again.

We must have integrity as a company in order to maintain credibility. Employees are loyal to organizations that follow through with their purpose. Customers want to and will buy from brands that have their back—brands that are living their purpose of making the world better by reducing harm.

WHAT PURPOSEFUL COMMUNICATION ISN'T

When our DEI work strays from purpose, it becomes aimless, inauthentic, and ungrounded. People quickly stop believing us because it feels like everything we say comes from nowhere—mere tactics at best, and at worst, theater. The gap between what we're doing and what we're saying widens every time our company drifts further from its purpose. This is a vicious cycle, peppered with red flags—like not using inclusive language, reinforcing negative stereotypes in our branding, and not paying employees a livable wage, all while saying the "right" things to the community in that International Women's Day post.

Public relations agencies tend to have multiple clients. They can make broad, sweeping recommendations on a particular social justice response with templated emails for clients and advice to say nothing or take no position. When articles publish leaked emails about this advice, the articles sometimes cite the PR firm's mission and use screenshots from social media posts during cultural moments to demonstrate how the firm says one thing but is not consistent through its actions. If we say we stand for something, we must live that purpose in the work we do for our clients, full stop. If we are a branding agency and we aren't helping our clients connect the dots between the brand and DEI, we are doing a disservice to our clients. We have to catch up and be there to guide our clients into a purposeful future.

Part of that guiding is helping both employees and leaders live the mission and values. We do that by inviting everyone to jump in and be involved via the inclusive content we create, disseminated through the inclusive channels we choose. We create with purpose to help everyone live with purpose.

Living with purpose means changing behavior at scale: leaders role-modeling the company's mission and vision, and employees providing the momentum. It's about everyone at every level taking the company's purpose seriously, in tangible, meaningful ways. DEI cannot be delegated.

In this day and age, no one has patience for excuses. We're not going to get away with dishonesty. It will come out. So, own the narrative based on truth rather than spinning, and have integrity. Be honest, be proactive, be upfront, and be purposeful.

PURPOSEFUL COMMUNICATION IN ACTION

If you stand for nothing, Burr, what'll you fall for?

—**Hamilton,** *the musical*

A company's purpose is supposed to be so audacious that it will likely never get accomplished in our lifetimes. It gives employees and leaders something to work for, and it fuels intentional progress as they go. Below are just a few examples:

- GoDaddy's™ Vision: GoDaddy's vision and mission is to radically shift the global economy toward life-fulfilling independent ventures. We do that by helping our customers kick ass—giving them the tools, insights, and the people to transform their ideas and personal initiative into success, however they measure it.

- Wikipedia's Vision: A world in which every single person is given free access to the sum of all human knowledge.

- Ben & Jerry's™ Three-Part Mission:
  - ▷ Product Mission: To make, distribute, and sell the finest quality ice cream and euphoric concoctions with a continued commitment to incorporating wholesome, natural ingredients and promoting business practices that respect the earth and the environment.

  - ▷ Economic Mission: To operate the company on a sustainable financial basis of profitable growth, increasing value for our stakeholders, and expanding opportunities for development and career growth for our employees.

  - ▷ Social Mission: To operate the company in a way that actively recognizes the central role that business plays in society by initiating innovative ways to improve the quality of life locally, nationally, and internationally.

THE PURPOSEFUL COMMUNICATOR

We wear many hats in helping our organizations become purposeful. At first, it's all about accentuating the core capabilities of our company. So, what are those core capabilities? Something we know better than anybody else. Many are obvious, some are more subtle. Are there areas within core capabilities that serve the purpose and contribute to resolving social inequities? Consider the UPS Operation Warp Speed example earlier. For another example, if we're a survey company, we may know how to do surveys, ask questions, and make our surveys accessible in different languages. But how do we tie in content that drives human-centric, meaningful conversations through surveys? How do we express our core capability in connecting people and creating better conversations for customers, employees, and society in general?

We'll also be called on to put together a communications strategy that aligns with the company's purpose. This means we first have to define that purpose, which includes the mission and vision, and then gut-check ourselves every time we're drafting communications. Build a creative brief as part of embedding DEI into the communications process.

Ask, "Is this aligning with our purpose? Is this furthering our purpose? Is it helping us move forward? Is it helping us make progress in this area, this grandiose idea that we have of why we uniquely exist in the world and how we want to make the world better?" Then as a communicator, we are consistent in following up with progress on those commitments we've outlined—internal dashboard, internal newsletters, company meetings, and employee resource groups (ERGs), for example. It needs to be a mix of channels to make sure everybody sees the progress and knows how they can participate. We communicate in the spaces where our people already are. We go to them.

And if we encounter pushback or need to make a case to our leaders for purposeful communication? It should be an easy sell, as our mission and vision statements have already been carefully crafted and implemented. The only question to ask is, "Does this situation align with our purpose?"

The purpose of a corporation, remember, is to benefit all stakeholders. This translates into making the world a better place, which includes standing for human, animal, and nature's rights to exist. Employees are humans and rights are the basics to exist.

One way to further clarify our sense of purpose is to ask ourselves if we're commenting or committing. We need to respond in a way that aligns with our purpose, our capabilities, and our values. If we have nothing to offer that supports disability rights, for example, we don't have a lot of ground to stand on. We will be performative. We should represent what is honestly happening in the company. We can comment, which a lot of organizations choose to do if they don't have an authentic connection to the issue at hand. We can and should say, "What happened was awful/unacceptable." However, this needs to be done in an educated way, as we talked about earlier. For instance, if you're not Black or African American in the United States, don't say that you're "shocked" when something like George Floyd's murder happens, because it isn't actually shocking to someone who is Black and has grown up in the U.S. To say that we're shocked means that we are unaware of the social and historical context and the magnitude of something happening. Comment only when we can do so in a way that makes it clear that we have done our homework and have representation in our network—experts and people with lived experiences—who are willing to share and help.

If we're not commenting, then we're committing. The first thing a lot of organizations will do to show their support is write a check. This can definitely help. However, it's a more purposeful move to follow through with action and communicate regularly on progress—even when there are learnings, mistakes, and failures along the way. People respect people more when they see them as human, fallible, and owning their mistakes. Same with companies.

Build relationships with the organizations we give checks to. Work to reduce any harm, making sure the company isn't contributing to the very systemic issues the nonprofit is trying to dismantle. One of our superpowers is visibility, and visibility drives accountability. Do what you can from where you are with what you have. Don't center the organization as a hero or savior. Instead, center the people impacted and align company action with the company mission. Finally, involve employees in the work so they can further educate themselves and build relationships in their community and beyond.

COMMUNICATING WITH DEPTH: GETTING PURPOSEFUL

Keep these three C's in mind when investigating whether or not communication is purposeful, and where we might become even better aligned with our purpose in future communications.

1. CONSIDER: **Position** the purpose.

    Make sure there is a clear connection between the situation and the purpose of the organization.

    Considered question: Is this aligned with the company's mission (and vision)?

2. CLARIFY: **Promote** the purpose.

    Center the people your organization serves as part of the people impacted by the situation.

    Clarified statement: This is how the message supports our mission and advances our vision.

3. COMMUNICATE: **Publicize** the purpose.

Incorporate the mission into the message so the connection is clear.

Committed action: Our mission to XYZ calls on us to do LMNOP.

KEY TAKEAWAYS

1. Stay aligned to the organization's mission, vision, and purpose, always.

2. To be purposeful, position, promote, and publicize the mission and vision.

3. Be clear on whether you're commenting or committing.

Communicating with Purpose

by Vikki Conwell

> *Authentic leadership is revealed in the alignment of*
> *what you think, what you say, and what you do.*

—Michael Holland, executive coach

In the aftermath of the George Floyd murder and consequential social unrest, corporations rushed to demonstrate their wokeness. They wrote DEI charters, issued statements, and pledged financial support to communities and institutions of color. Organizations large and small even rebranded themselves as mission-driven to align with America's seemingly renewed social consciousness.

Two years and a global pandemic later, most of these businesses have failed to become diverse and inclusive, neglected to honor their promised philanthropy, and continued operating siloed from any social mission or purpose. Instead, many sought the public benefits of stating a position rather than committing to one.

But here's a reality check: Not every business wants to be mission-or purpose-driven, nor do they seek to operate with a high degree of integrity. Unfortunately, doing so requires more culture and organizational change than some leaders are willing to implement. So, they opt for performative behavior—checking the diversity boxes, echoing the right buzzwords and phrases, and donating dollars to causes—to appear woke without waking up.

The misalignment between what companies say and do erodes their credibility. As the credibility gap widens, so does the trust that people—especially their employees—have in these institutions. Despite an expressed desire to trust their leadership, many employees cannot connect the dots between organizational purpose and practice, specifically in their roles.

When the Business Roundtable challenged corporations to lead with purpose, 79% of business leaders agreed that purpose was integral to their success. Unfortunately, the memo didn't trickle down to employees, as most remain ill-equipped to answer the why and how. An alarming 59% of American workers do not genuinely understand what their employer stands for, why it matters, and what it means for their job performance, according to Gallup®'s research. They just don't get it, or they don't buy it. Possibly both.

So, how do communicators help companies restore trust, operationalize purpose, and transform intent into action? Authenticity and accountability.

Authenticate the Commitment

Aligning purpose to performance requires a willingness to change. A communication professional cannot compel an organization to become anything it's not willing to become. So, check for a genuine and robust commitment to change from leadership.

Organizations that are authentically driven by a clear mission and purpose align their words and actions all the time. These organizations communicate openly, honestly, and consistently with internal and external audiences about their purpose until it permeates the organization's DNA. All of its communication will reflect this commitment.

More than just words on digital paper, communication around purpose creates synergy among stakeholders towards a bigger mission. Also, this language helps employees at every level of the organization take ownership of overall performance and success, which leads to increased engagement, job satisfaction, and retention.

Communicating about purpose also correlates to speaking about performance and profitability. Studies have shown that people want to work for and spend their money with organizations they view as purpose- and value-driven. In addition, the stock of corporations deemed as purposeful reportedly performs better, and corporations listed among the World's Most Ethical Companies also outperformed comparable businesses by 7% over five years.

Stop the Buck Here

An organization's reputation rests on the shoulders of its leadership. The CEO's ability to communicate a clear vision internally and externally, model desired behavior, and set clear expectations for standards/ethics, impact reputation more than increasing shareholder value or executing the strategic vision.

In a survey conducted by IBM®, 60% of CEOs expressed a strong desire to engage employees around shared values, purpose, and mission—the employer attributes that post-pandemic job seekers value even more now. They lean on communicators to help them articulate their organization's vision, goals, and measures of success.

Likewise, as the reputation manager and author of organizational messaging, communication professionals share responsibility for aligning communication with purpose and vision. We often have the ear of leadership and serve as the initial sounding board for new concepts, practices, and theories of change. We craft the messages around a shared vision and strategy that empowers and engages employees, builds trust, and increases brand awareness; thus, we should hold the organization accountable for making the messaging matter. It's our duty.

Just Freakin' Ask

Undoubtedly, trying to hold an organization, especially a large enterprise, accountable for aligning its work with its words creates a herculean task for any communication professional. So, don't try to do it all. Instead, make an impact where and how you can, beginning with a few well-placed questions:

- ► How does this initiative support the organization's vision and mission?
- ► How does this campaign align with our purpose?
- ► Is this initiative consistent with our brand?
- ► How can we ensure its success?

These thought starters prompt leaders to pause, establish benchmarks, and contemplate how to monitor their effectiveness. They challenge leaders to consider the cost of making statements without clear implementation strategies. Such questions can help ensure that written words turn into action.

Be forewarned that asking challenging questions will not win the communication professional any congeniality awards or popularity contests. Internal stakeholders might try to circumvent the processes and practices, but eventually, their initial discomfort will give rise to real transformational change. Communicators have the power to influence purposeful change; exert it.

Biography

Vikki Conwell (she/her) is a corporate communications consultant and social impact strategist who helps organizations articulate the alignment of their mission and their market. The former journalist asks the tough questions to challenge conventional thinking, disclose the real issues, and clearly communicate what matters most. She advocates for equity and inclusion and against racism and injustice.

CHAPTER 7

T IS FOR TAILORED

In a time where the world is becoming personalized,
when the mobile phone, the burger, everything has its
own personal identity, how should we perceive ourselves
and how should we perceive others?

—Al-Mayassa bint Hamad bin
Khalifa Al-Thani, philanthropist

Tailoring is a step that many of us miss when it comes to communication. We move from company to company, hoping what we've done at previous jobs works at our new organization. We may even call it "best practices." But it's a new day, a new role, and a new context with different people, customers, and goals. To stay safe while trying to make an immediate impact, we'll put together messaging with neato-sounding words that might inspire without moving people to action because the message is broad, diluted, and lacking "teeth."

WHAT IS TAILORED COMMUNICATION?

Tailored communication is when we take purpose to the next level by asking, "Do we have the credibility to be talking about or doing this? Is this an issue that we can move the needle on—uniquely?" In other words, are we in our lane here? Is this in any way attached to what we do? As an organization, we must connect to our core competencies, skills, and expertise. Our messaging should add to the knowledge base and demonstrate that what we do has a meaningful impact that is specific and unique. No one can say what we say, do what we do. We own this space. In well-tailored communication, we also bring different messages to different stakeholders, customizing them so they reflect and resonate with the company culture. They all need to hear different things. This is not the same as telling them what they want to hear, but rather, crafting the message to meet the different interests and needs of investors, employees, customers, the larger world, and so on. Each time we tailor communication for a different stakeholder, it should have both the feel and the content that only the organization can bring.

HOW CONSCIOUS COMMUNICATION IS TAILORED

Consider the difference between tailored clothing and mass-produced fast fashion. A tailor measures you, then shortens, lengthens, or tightens the clothing to fit. Fast fashion is one-size fits most, sometimes baggy, sometimes tight, seldom just right. The same is true of communications.

One-size-fits all—as it relates to our communication—is messaging anybody could create. It's not special or unique to our brand or our organization. Anybody can say "thoughts and prayers," which means little to the intended audience. Anybody can spill jargon and acronyms that negate listening. It's easy, it doesn't take any effort.

Trying to make one message meaningful to everyone makes it meaningful to no one. When we understand each of our stakeholders' unique needs, we can create a message that resonates with each of them. We never can assume everyone will understand or even read one message, sent one way. Distribution mix is key. Go where the stakeholders already are.

Tailor who sends the message as well. Not all messages are external (but plan that they will be) and not all internal messages have to come from the CEO or head of DEI. Different leaders have different personal investments, expertise, or experience in different situations, and may be able to speak more effectively to a particular stakeholder. In fact, messaging coming from a broad set of people within the employee base shows widespread commitment to action.

WHY TAILORED COMMUNICATION IS BENEFICIAL

The biggest good here is increased visibility for the company. A tailored message better educates people on what the company does, who it is, and what it stands for. Owning a space positions the company to communicate from a place of strength, expanding the knowledge about an issue with its unique industry experience, customer insight, or deep research. It's an incredible opportunity to tell the company story while centering on an impacted population and leveraging privilege, power, and agency to educate and drive action for meaningful progress. Our companies have tremendous power, and there's a void we can fill by defining the character of the organization by our actions.

WHAT TAILORED COMMUNICATION ISN'T

It is not always easy to spot when communication isn't tailored. Even fast fashion can fit in a pinch, even if it doesn't express our unique personality and place in the world. This meme humorously expresses the predicament of generic communication:[47]

---

[47] Chris Franklin Tweet: https://twitter.com/campster/status/1267183124582215680?lang=en.

A statement from [Brand]®

We at [Brand] are committed to fighting
injustice by posting images to Twitter that express our
commitment to fighting injustice.

To that end, we offer this solemn white-on-black .jpeg that
expresses vague solidarity with the Black community, but will
quietly elude the specifics of what is wrong, what needs to
change, or in what ways we will do anything about it. This is
doubly true if [Brand] is particularly guilty of exacerbating
these issues.

We hope this action encourages you to view [Brand]
positively without, you know, expecting anything from us.

[BRAND]®

You know the ones.™

12:56 PM · May 31, 2020 · TweetDeck

When we don't tailor our messages, readers won't connect to the content. It will be boring, likely full of corporate-speak, and unbelievable (not in a good way, simply because people won't believe it). We can test ourselves anytime by replacing our organization's name with another organization from a completely different industry. If it still works, then it's not tailored.

Tailored communication is not softened language. Traditionally, we used to avoid saying much at all or hiding the fact that we don't know what we're talking about. Softening language means choosing "safer" or more generic words to make people more comfortable with our statements. Conscious communicators using The DEPTH Model can challenge this approach and opt, instead, to call a thing a thing. We can choose wording that is accurate, appropriate, and authentic to the situation. We don't have to google random Martin Luther King, Jr.

quotes to help the CEO sound smart and end up missing the whole point of what we're commenting on. We can do the work ahead of time to understand the context well enough to tell the difference between a protest and an insurrection. We will call a thing a thing.

TAILORED COMMUNICATION IN ACTION

Take this example from Boston Scientific:

> At Boston Scientific, diversity, equity, and inclusion (DE&I) means fostering an environment where people of all cultures, ethnicities, gender identities, backgrounds, experiences, orientations, and beliefs can be themselves as they work together to advance science for life.
>
> We want everyone to feel they belong and be engaged and empowered to share new ideas and perspectives. This is essential to our values-driven culture, our focus on innovation, equality, and enabling our people to thrive and succeed. When people can bring their authentic selves to work, it drives the diversity of thought that elevates collaboration and leads to our greatest breakthroughs for patients around the world.
>
> In addition to guiding all internal policies and practices, our commitment to DE&I extends to our external activities, including advocating for health equity and making meaningful contributions to accelerate inclusion in our society."[48]

The tailored part of this statement is what Boston Scientific knows, learns, and is a part of improving: healthcare. They start with what they do and commit to advocating for health equity. This statement would not apply to a bank or grocery store chain. It cannot be cut and pasted to apply to any company in any industry. If our culture uses less company

---

[48] "Diversity & Inclusion—Careers." n.d. www.bostonscientific.com.

jargon, we can adjust to a more conversational style. If our brand can be more specific on actions, then we should be.

Here's another example from the Dallas Mavericks (professional men's basketball team):

> Born out of a need to create sustainable, lasting change, in June 2020, the Dallas Mavericks launched Mavs Take ACTION!, a plan to address racial inequalities, promote social justice, and drive change within Dallas/Fort Worth.
>
> Standing strong in the belief that every voice matters and everybody belongs, Mavs Take ACTION! focuses on six systems inclusive of Public Policy, Education, Criminal Justice, Employment, Child Welfare, and Healthcare, with initiatives across six key pillars of Advocacy, Communication, Training, Investment, Outreach, and Noise, or ACTION![49]

As a professional basketball team, the Dallas Mavericks know where they can make a difference and spell it out in a specific plan. They aren't trying to be something they are not. They see the opportunities within their reach, claim them, and take action. By sharing externally, this visibility drives accountability.

THE TAILORED COMMUNICATOR

There used to be a time when it was much harder to say stupid sh*t on our own because the media was a platform we did not control. As that shifts and continues to shift, there are many more unknowns; we're in a much more dynamic space. Tailoring messages for a myriad of stakeholders positions us as thought leaders. We can make it simple for our people. "Does it involve a diverse group?" If the answer is yes,

[49] "Mavs Take Action!" The Official Home of the Dallas Mavericks. n.d. https://www.mavs.com/mavstakeaction/.

go through The DEPTH Model and then run it past people impacted by the issue and message created to address it.

There is a specific type of pushback that we can expect when trying to tailor our communications, and it has to do with companies that have not yet truly defined their lane or purpose. When this happens, some people may want to go broader and say things like, "This is what our competitors are saying, what other people in our industry are saying, so let's say the same thing." Let them know that they are missing out on a huge opportunity to be distinct, stand out, and be meaningful in the dialogue.

Keeping up with other companies on a topic is not good enough. Our company spends a lot of money on sales and marketing to be distinct in the marketplace, convincing customers that we are the best and only choice. DEI messaging deserves the same tailoring, nothing less.

COMMUNICATING WITH DEPTH: BEING TAILORED

Keep these three C's in mind when investigating whether or not the communication is tailored, and where we might ensure an even better fit for the audience in future communications.

1. CONSIDER: **Take** stock of capabilities.

   Ensure the message is something you can speak to from a position of strength and expertise, and help the reader see that it makes sense that you're sending this message.

   Considered question: Is this in our lane?

2. CLARIFY: **Tailor** your message.

   The message can't be generic and something that can be pasted into anyone else's message. Make it clear what business you're in.

   Clarified statement: We are uniquely positioned to do XYZ/we are different because LMNOP.

3. COMMUNICATE: **Tell** your story.

Expand the knowledge with what your company can uniquely do. Be specific and actionable.

Committed action: We are in the unique position to XYZ because we LMNOP.

KEY TAKEAWAYS

1. Highlight the organization's unique competencies, strengths, and influences.

2. Tailor messages by audience and sender.

3. Tell the company's unique story.

The Joy of Being Seen

by Chelsea Delaney

I am autistic. You can't separate me from my autism and I'm not looking for a way to do so. It's not insulting to call me autistic any more than it is to call me tall, even though I was made to believe it was for years as a teacher. We were constantly pushed towards language like, "on the spectrum," or, "person with autism." It was only much later, after my own diagnosis, that I had to start repairing the harm caused by that wording, the deep wound of being made invisible to myself.

So you better believe I was excited when I saw an ad this April, more widely known as Autism Awareness Month, that looked me directly in the eye (which I usually hate, but didn't mind because it was an ad). The company makes tactile processing fidgets for a variety of people who are seeking relief from high anxiety. Through this ad, they were giving away free samples of this fidget with each purchase in April. This, in and of itself, shows a basic level of doing their homework on their audience—they know they make a product that a group might use, and so they give it away for that awareness month. I was intrigued.

Then, with the help of conscious communicators, they were able to go one step further. Many in this community are advocating away from the title of Autism Awareness Month, towards Autism Acceptance Month. The reasoning for this shift goes, "Aren't we aware enough of autism already?" Thus this company used "Autism Acceptance Month," in big, bold letters, smack dab in the middle of their visual. They also used identity-first language (*autistic person* rather than *person with autism*) three different times in the ad—twice in the copy, and once in the ad itself. Now I was downright giddy.

It would have been easy for them to run with generic and outdated language, and perhaps even evoked less discomfort for people who are not autistic. However, the ad's word choices not only made autistic people feel seen, but subtly pushed at one of many stereotypes surrounding autism: autistic people as either simpletons or geniuses. Though there are autistic people who need extra help, and those who have extraordinary skills, there are also plenty of them who are neither. Some autistic people just do mundane, everyday tasks like go to work, pay bills, and buy things that they need for their wellness and self-care. I am damn capable of buying my own fidgets, thank you very much.

People commenting on this ad were *exuberant* with gratitude at being addressed in a way where they felt seen. In fact, I didn't even see comments about the actual product 'til 30 comments down in the thread. What's more, in the weeks to come, I saw autistic people reshare this same ad on multiple social media groups for neurodivergent people that I belong to. It's like we were all at the zoo, gathered gape-mouthed around some exotic animal. The relief and awe at not being re-traumatized in April was palpable. From one small act of compassionate tailoring, this company sustained and increased their visibility and brand loyalty. More importantly, they helped undo a tiny bit of the harm that is so easily done when we're not paying attention to who's in front of us.

Biography

Chelsea Delaney (he/him) is an artist, writer, and editor (a.k.a. a believer in impossible things). He works primarily in mixed media and acrylic and brings his love of color and storytelling into helping others find, craft, and tell their stories. Diagnosed autistic late in life, he feels lucky to also work with families with neurodivergent young people. Find his work or contact him on newstoriescalling.com.

Be consistent.

CHAPTER 8

H IS FOR HABITUAL

First, forget inspiration. Habit is more dependable.
Habit will sustain you whether you're inspired or not.

—Octavia Butler, author

As communicators, we need to be aware of what our habits are in how we handle DEI and social justice communications. Is it our habit to handle the most recent crisis and then go back to business as usual? Is it our habit to only talk about Latine/Hispanic folks in September and October in the U.S.? Is it our habit to speak up when our competitors do or when there's social capital to be gained? What are we expecting employees and customers to trust about us? Inconsistency can erode trust. Conscious communication is consistent.

WHAT IS HABITUAL COMMUNICATION?

Habitual communication is where it all comes together. Is this something we have talked about before or intend to address going forward?

We can be deliberate, educated, purposeful, and tailor our work to have the greatest impact in the sphere we occupy, but it can fall apart quickly if the practice does not become innate to the way our organization does business. This doesn't mean all is lost. Messes *will* happen and *can* be cleaned up using The DEPTH Model, but habitual practice will save us from constant and drastic mess.

At its core, habitual DEI work is both consistent and continual. Much of the energy for this ongoing conversation comes from a strong connection to an organization's vision and mission. This gives us the resources we need to be proactive and the commitment to sustain what we start. Anyone can celebrate Native American Heritage Month in November. Anyone can respond to the crisis of another Black man being murdered. However, as we mentioned earlier, one-off actions are merely band-aids covering a deeply wounded system. Truly transformational DEI work must be built on a foundation that allows it to be habitual.

Sustainability is also key here, and there are many ways to help our organization keep the work going. When we step out on a DEI issue and into the social justice space, we need to step out with some accountability. What will the company say about this issue a week from now, a month from now, a year from now? Accountability becomes real when the actions we commit to are specific and deliverable.

There are three types of accountability that we can and should practice:

1. *Celebration:* Be present in celebration, yes, absolutely. Visibility, raising awareness, representation, pride, support, and education are very important. However, if we stop with just this level of practice, as most organizations do, we are performative by default. Explore the next type of accountability to become more intentional.

2. *Crisis:* Be there in crisis where rights are suppressed and physical/mental/spiritual safety are not guaranteed. Look internally to where we are not paid equitably, benefits are insufficient, promotion and performance haven't been overhauled, and systems and processes rebuilt. We don't get to just celebrate and then ignore the systems, issues, etc. that continue to hold us back and limit our health, safety, human rights, wealth, potential, and happiness.

3. *Consistent:* Don't just talk about DEI and social justice during a heritage month or on an awareness day. We have to embed DEI into our daily existence, not just due to an external crisis or when society chooses to highlight it. This is where we build our proof points and learn along the way.

HOW CONSCIOUS COMMUNICATION IS HABITUAL

Businesses have to consistently deliver on their brand promises. Our leaders are accountable for setting goals for the business. Our products and services should be available in our markets in a way that is accessible to our customers. In short, the areas of our businesses that are already consistent are those that are intentionally measured. In contrast, communications are often under-measured, under-resourced, and inconsistent. That's not good enough for the next evolution of our businesses and organizations. All of these areas that are measured include forms of communication, and thus communications teams in our companies deserve the same resources, investments, and standards of measurement necessary to create and sustain ongoing DEI habits.

To make our conscious communications more habitual, we must become aware of our habits. If resources and measurements help us achieve goals and brand promises, then why aren't we using the same habits for DEI? What habit is keeping us from using these best practices in all areas of our organization? Once we understand this, we can begin to change our habits, giving new habits a real chance to take root in the face of expectations, distractions, and unconscious bias. It requires incredible awareness to help us both own and manage this habit change. Whether it is through consultants, colleagues, or companies that have been habitual in their storytelling for a long time, there are lots of choices for whom to call on.

Joy Harjo, the 23rd Poet Laureate of the United States and writer of the Muscogee (Creek) Nation said, "A story matrix connects all of us. There are rules, processes, and circles of responsibility in this world. And the story begins exactly where it is supposed to begin. We cannot skip any part."[50] When we're committing to change, we're making a promise in the now for a better future. To hold both the now and the future in the present is a huge undertaking, but not impossible, and it's what our employees, our customers, and our larger world deserve. We can only make a decision that creates a better future when we are in alignment with that commitment.

WHY HABITUAL COMMUNICATION IS BENEFICIAL

Once our organization starts making DEI an everyday part of how we do business, we'll start to see a drop in the amount of time we spend on the back foot, continually reacting to whatever crisis is next. Doesn't that feel great just to read and imagine? That is the reason we create habits in the first place—to conserve energy that can then be freed up to go to other places it is needed. In fact, Charles Duhigg, who has written extensively on the science of habit formation, writes, "Once a behavior becomes automatic, it is regulated by a different part of the brain that is associated with less effort, less depletion of resources."[51] Wow! Our

---

[50] Harjo, Joy. *Crazy Brave: A Memoir*. W. W. Norton & Company, 2012.

[51] "The Power of Habit." The Washington Center for Cognitive Therapy.

organization's new habits may seem costly to sustain in the beginning, but we are actually resting a part of our "company brain" when we do so.

Bottom line: when our DEI practice is truly habitual, it is no longer a program, but rather a characteristic of our organization's communication.

WHAT HABITUAL COMMUNICATION ISN'T

So, what is the opposite of habitual communication? The week after George Floyd was murdered, Black creators in the music industry initiated a campaign entitled Blackout Tuesday to raise awareness about police brutality and systemic racism. Instagram users quickly took up the movement, posting black squares, many of them hashtagged with #BlackLivesMatter. Soon there were calls from actual Black Lives Matter activists letting people know that they'd posted so many squares that much of the content they were trying to get out to people about fundraising and protests was being obscured. Not only that, but nine states and Washington D.C. were having primary elections that day. This made it a challenging day for people to promise to go offline. Then companies appropriated the black squares, clogging up feeds with copycat, empty statements. Ugh.

This is an excellent example of communication that is not habitual. Reactive and performative strategies may vent steam in a crisis situation, but they don't lead to long-lasting transformation and aren't sustainable. The instant gratification and heightened emotionality of social media often disguise the harm done by trendy campaigns. While social media can be a part of our DEI work, it cannot be the whole strategy. Ultimately, it is hollow, because it is not connected to a larger vision—we're being reactive, and we don't have a legacy of content and proof points to point to. That all happened because of the intersection of immediacy and simplicity. We know how to make a black box with white text, however, compacting very complex social and historical situations into a few words severely dilutes the true work to be done.

Remember, employees pay attention and they see the pattern. If we are talking about standing in solidarity with the Black community in reaction to George Floyd's murder, you can bet Asian folks, women of all identities, Latine/Hispanic folks, and LGBTQ+ folks are watching and wondering if we will be there for them too when (not if) tragedy strikes their community. By the way, "standing in solidarity" isn't helpful. Just standing isn't progress, we've gotta move. We've seen tragedies and crises happen in other communities, and we are not there for them in our messaging, storytelling, listening sessions, donations, and training. We need to make the effort to make progress for our employees' rights when they are threatened and especially when they are restricted or eliminated.

HABITUAL COMMUNICATION IN ACTION

We have so many chances to make DEI habitual on a day-to-day basis. Why not publish a story in December about Anti-Asian Hate, instead of only during Asian American Heritage Month in May? Let's provide content and stories involving intersectionality, such as someone who is Black, transgender, a veteran, autistic, and Muslim during Pride month in June. These are some examples of communications that demonstrate consistency. Talking about a population and keeping their experiences at the top of our minds helps us better understand the historical and social context without an external factor such as a cultural moment, heritage month, awareness day, or social justice crisis.

Habit, or lack thereof, is also on display whenever our company gives its money to problematic non-profit organizations and political support. If our companies have a habit of changing the company logo to a rainbow version in June for Pride month and donating company money to the Human Rights Commission (HRC), meanwhile the company's Political Action Committee (PAC)[52] is giving money

---

[52] "Political Action Committees." Open Secrets. Accessed June 4, 2022. https://www.opensecrets.org/political-action-committees-pacs/2022.

to politicians who are involved in anti-LGBTQ+ rights laws, voter suppression initiatives, or anti-women's rights laws, that's a problem. Do the due diligence to understand the company's involvement with those outside the company. Whom and what do these entities stand for, and what are they doing with the support the company gives them? Also, for PR folks, be proactive in understanding your C-suite's past and present personal and professional donation habits, and be prepared for questions if behavior and money are at cross purposes to DEI statements and company values.

Traditionally, the line we tend to use to explain political donations is to say we support those who support our company interests. Most would agree that's important—until they discover that thousands and even millions of dollars are going to people who are restricting or taking away basic human rights, causing human rights violations, and causing harm to the planet when our company has pledged to be more environmentally responsible, act in solidarity with a population, etc. When we have the habit of running our business at cross purposes and without integrity, the communicator's job becomes exponentially more difficult.

If a change is worth making and sustaining, it will often encounter pushback to comfort zones and the status quo. So, how do we make a case to leaders and decision-makers to embrace habitual DEI? There are so many other priorities competing for attention and resources—how do we get them to stay the course? Simply put, we have to demonstrate the cost of not being habitual.

Performative DEI can wreck a reputation that took years to build, in an instant. That reputation can take years to rebuild. That may not mean a lot at first glance, but there is a monetary cost to a bad reputation. A report published by a stakeholder intelligence firm said, "A bad reputation also speaks to staffing, a major percentage of any business's costs. Some 84% of employees would consider quitting in favour of an offer from a company with a great reputation, and research by the

Harvard Business Review with ICM Unlimited found that a company with 10,000 employees and a bad reputation could be spending $7.6m in additional wages to counter it. That's around $4,723 per hire."[53] That is a hard number to ignore, especially in trying economic times. If your decision-makers don't want to fund consistent efforts, ask them to think about whether or not they can afford the hit to the company's bottom line when they don't.

THE HABITUAL COMMUNICATOR

Communicators are key in helping organizations become habitual. First and foremost, we gather and create the resources needed to be sustainable and consistent. This may come in the form of internal or external relationships, infrastructure, editorial calendars, co-creating with ERGs, inviting in grassroots groups, and weighing in on the budget itself. There is an opportunity here for us to change our own habits around how we resource initiatives. How much are we taking for granted? How much opportunity are we missing by just doing what we did last year and buying more wristbands and t-shirts rather than investing in consultants, speakers, listening sessions, and experiential opportunities to be in the work itself? Are we continuing listening sessions and bringing in speakers and trainers even when there isn't a social justice crisis? How are we demonstrating ongoing learning?

There are skills needed to build and protect a habitual core capability for our DEI communications. First, we need people who will own and manage their position. This is someone who doesn't wait for others to come and ask why we aren't doing anything about the needs and issues of historically marginalized employees and customers. We plan the calendar with everyone in mind and then stick to it.

---

[53] "How to measure the cost of a bad reputation." Alva Group. Accessed December 12, 2021. https://www.alva-group.com/blog/how-to-measure-the-cost-of-a-bad-reputation/.

Next, we need people who will maneuver proactively. That looks like including DEI in our calendars and budgets, as well as building trust in our internal relationships and external experts. Basically, it means getting our network in place before we enter the work in a haphazard fashion. Finally, we communicate the importance of habitual DEI by maintaining sustainability. Don't let our stories get bumped or our budgets get co-opted. There is a lot we are responsible for saying on a daily basis. Don't lose sight of the focus. Avoid short-sightedness and remember the big picture.

Traditional communications will argue that we can't say something about everything, every time. Maybe, maybe not. That's the beauty of The DEPTH Model—to know when, where, how, and why to say something. Again, more can be said internally when we empower our ERGs, diversity councils, executive sponsors, and other champions; they can take ownership of the events and cultural moments they are a part of, and they can be the ones sharing knowledge, inviting employees to learn and grow in their understanding. We democratize cultural moments by having an internal channel for those who are part of those moments to share, teach, and celebrate. Corporate communications should not be the authority of what should and shouldn't be recognized. Let the community speak for themselves, involve them, and hand them the mic consistently. Side note: if someone needs a quick example of bias in companies, take a look at the company holiday calendar and ask, who decided this and why? Actually, the answer is probably obvious.

Take Ramadan for example. Someone who participates in Ramadan can share the history, context, practices, effects of employees who are participating, and appropriate ways to greet someone who is practicing the tradition with respect. The CEO doesn't have to make a statement, especially if Ramadan is not a part of their practice. This is where internal and external relationships are helpful as the content is coming from someone who is personally involved and can share their experience. When we step aside and give the mic to someone else, it makes room for voices not often heard, from people previously invisible, and by default we all bear witness to authentic sharing and benefit from being educated. We don't have to do it all. We must build the network, channels, and guidelines, and defer to the people who know more than us.

George Floyd's murder wasn't a one-off, now-let's-just-go-back-to-normal, event. It was one moment in a long history and movement. Our habits will show history where we stand and history is being written right now, every day. If we have a habit of only saying a message when it's externally pressured—a crisis or a cultural moment (heritage month or awareness day)—it means our company's reputation is that we're like everyone else. We are continuing to say one thing and do another. We *are* just like everyone else.

That'll make it harder and harder to attract talent, have better representation throughout the levels of our organization, keep Generation Z and millennial employees and customers, avoid litigation from harassment and discrimination, innovate, and eventually compete. Neglecting to address these issues makes our communications irrelevant. When our communications don't resonate, it's a sign that our organization is becoming out of touch.

We are called on to be very persistent during this time of preparing for and growing new habits. On the preparation side, we have to put our foot down over and over again when people within our organization try to rush the process. A crisis is not the first time to enter the social justice space on an issue. Once the habit has started to take root, we must track and fine-tune until the policies and procedures are automatic. According to a 2009 study published in the European Journal of Social Psychology, it takes 18 to 254 days for a person to form a new habit. The study also concluded that, on average, it takes 66 days for a new behavior to become automatic.[54] If this is true of one person, imagine the implications at an organizational level. Holding the cognitive dissonance of that many people for so long takes persistence and tremendous resilience. And it's worth it.

As with all of the steps in The DEPTH Model, we have to make advanced decisions. Decisions and choices about our channels, our content, our editorial calendar, and our images to build our reputation and legacy seen and experienced within our communications. Make the decision to make DEI and social justice a habit in communications. It's work we can be proud of, and it'll take away that gut knot we feel when we knew we were putting something stupid out in the world that was not going to land well. Decide. Choose. Make it a habit.

COMMUNICATING WITH DEPTH: BEING HABITUAL

Keep these three C's in mind when investigating whether or not the communication is habitual, and where we might have the opportunity to trade old habits for ones that give us the room to be less reactive.

1. CONSIDER: **Hone** your commitment.

    Question if you are communicating to keep up with competitors, reacting to an external factor, or are at a starting point where this is a pivot of greater commitment that you will sustain.

    Considered question: Is this something we have committed to before and are willing to continue?

---

[54] Frothingham, Scott. "How Long Does It Take for a New Behavior to Become Automatic?" Healthline Media. October 24, 2019.

2. CLARIFY: **Hold** the line.

Be with impacted audiences through the good times and the bad and show that you are not fair-weather organizations only telling positive stories during heritage months.

Clarified statement: We've said it before and we'll say it again.

3. COMMUNICATE: **Handle** your business.

Culture proof points and untold stories abound in your organization. Build the infrastructure to surface them, document them, and share them to establish consistency beyond only external forcing factors.

Committed action: What resources are needed to change our current habits?

KEY TAKEAWAYS

1. Jumping in on and/or co-opting a trend to look good is not cool. Break the habit.

2. Develop new habits to be consistent which means we'll keep learning more and getting better at being more impactful.

3. Hone the commitment, hold the line, and handle business.

Communications for Social Impact: More Than a Slogan

by Miriam Khalifa

The definition of a campaign—whether you're talking politics or marketing—is an organized course of action to achieve a goal. If companies are seeking to achieve their goals—be it positive, social impact on the larger community or inclusive, internal culture—the organized course of action to take them there can't be left out.

While I'm a DEI practitioner who is passionate about organizational change, I began my career in public opinion and political research. In that capacity, I learned a lot about the time and thought that goes into a campaign's messaging strategy. Public opinion polling falls under the broader category of market research, which is used to inform campaigns on what messaging will win—whether that be a marketing campaign or a public policy initiative.

The goal of this research is to understand your audience (or market) segments and their values. This information informs the campaign on how it can tap into those values using communications, regardless of whether the goal is to sell a product or get constituents to learn and care about an issue and then vote on it.

> ▸ The process starts with conducting research to define the target audiences. Then, various messaging strategies are tested on their ability to sway audiences by tying the initiative or product to what resonates with that group.

► In addition to customizing messaging for specific groups, strategic placement and delivery of these communications also help the campaign reach and resonate with its various desired audiences.

Here's what we can learn from their process: campaigns invest money and time in research and strategy in order to be conscious, tailored, and habitual about their messaging and ultimately, achieve their goals. Organizations should be doing the same for their diversity, equity, and inclusion communications.

One client organization I worked with was puzzled by the upset among its Black employees following the release of their solidarity statement after the murder of George Floyd. They took a stance—one that felt radical to some of their leadership—by announcing that they stood with the Black community.

Well, not only was this the first time the organization had ever communicated its position on an issue that has been going on for centuries, but leadership hadn't checked in on its Black staff or asked for their input. While they publicly said they supported the community, there was no effort to evaluate or address the impact the murder had on the organization's own employees. Staff were expected to show up to work and do their jobs as if nothing had happened with no opportunity to process the event or their feelings around it.

This is a perfect example of how a lack of strategy and inconsistent, reactive communications can be detrimental. The misalignment between the leadership's actions and the statement they released ended up reinforcing an already palpable distrust in the organization's ability to support their

Black employees, particularly during intense moments of visible injustice.

Companies use market research to inform their ad campaigns and generate sales, and candidates can win elections based on their messaging. It's time for organizations to utilize similar strategies for social justice initiatives if they are serious about going beyond performative communications and want to create real change. Organizations can instead use their platforms to create and reinforce positive impact.

Communication is necessary for making employees and the larger community aware of the work you are doing. While announcements help build momentum and excitement around your initiative, they can also serve as an accountability tool for your organization. Publicly stating that your company commits to a certain action requires habitual communications thereafter to keep the larger community informed and updated on the work you're doing. Bonus points for including a specific dollar amount (either raised or donated) or a date the organization will accomplish certain milestones by.

While you can tell the public what you want, or even plan to do, your company will find itself up against a brick wall if it doesn't have buy-in from the people needed to carry out your initiative. After all, your initiative will be deliverable because it sits within your company's area of expertise, so naturally, your employees will play a large part in carrying out the tasks to achieve those goals. Make sure that the majority of your company can see the end goal.

Communications need to be consistent, informative, and successfully tailored to their audiences in order to make employees feel invested in your initiative. Conscious and habitual communications can do more than just communicate follow-through on your company's commitments. They can also enhance accountability and increase the likelihood of achieving greater impact. When crafted well, they have the ability to reinforce and reinvigorate your company's mission and values by tying them to tangible actions involving the outside community.

Biography

Miriam Khalifa (she/her) is passionate about the power of communications and data to create organizational and social change. She began her career in political and public opinion research, shaping the messaging of top campaigns in the U.S. As a DEI strategist, she has leveraged communications and research to establish effective initiatives for diversity, equity, and inclusion. Currently, she does consulting and data analytics to optimize the impact of DEI strategies for financial services and technology companies.

SECTION 3
THE
INFRASTRUCTURE

CHAPTER 9

LEADING THE LEADERS

The art of communication is the language of leadership.

**—James Humes, author and
former presidential speechwriter**

Regardless of what leaders think personally, despite their true intent, when they speak, people listen. When they don't speak, people take notice. When they say stupid sh*t, people make it go viral. What leaders say or don't say affects the people they lead, the brands they stand for, and the legacies they work to build. For most people, the occasional misspeak is embarrassing. For leaders, misspeak can be devastating.

SURVEILLING SPEECH

When leaders speak, they generally mean well. Even if they don't, most are savvy enough to realize that what they say matters—especially when they say stupid sh*t. Yet, every day brings a new screw up, a new apology for a screw up, or a new need to double down on dumb because of a screw up.

Often, we just assume leaders know better. After all, they wouldn't get where they are without stellar communications skills, right? Wrong. And nobody knows this better than the communicators who support them. Ask any executive speechwriter. What they *won't* tell you is how much hand holding and pearl clutching is involved in shepherding a principal to uncover and own a story enough to share it authentically. Ask any communications officer charged with supporting a CEO or senior leadership team. They'll tell you about the late nights and early mornings needed to keep egos, expressions, and edicts from creating chaos and the emergency interventions needed to fix things. They'll explain why they don't give the CEO global email access.

But if leading leaders is a goat rodeo for the people working directly with them, what does it mean for communicators further from the corner office, but not so far as to escape the fallout from communications missteps? When leaders say the wrong things or fail to say the right ones, there are consequences and repercussions for communicators in all segments—internal, external, marketing, PR, social, investor. Because that's the thing: stupid sh*t rolls downhill.

MITIGATING MISSPEAK

What do we do when leaders say way too much or not nearly enough? It's helpful to start by thinking about what communication misspeaks look like in the first place and what might be behind them (spoiler alert: cognitive biases). Misspeak typically falls into one of four categories:

1. **Insensitive statements:** When leaders stop listening to what others think—be it ideas, criticism, or general opinions— they're subject to insensitive responses. Sometimes it's psychological hubris, the false-consensus effect, assuming that what

they believe is not only true but widely held as truth. Other times, they're suffering from confirmation bias, which the American Psychological Association defines as "the tendency to gather evidence that confirms preexisting expectations, typically by emphasizing or pursuing supporting evidence while dismissing or failing to seek contradictory evidence."[55] As author, organizational strategist, pragmatic theologian, and social capitalist Dr. Stephen R. Graves says, "in leadership, tone deafness is like a virus—you can get it through no fault of your own, but it's your response to it that determines how bad it gets."[56] Such was the case when a leader at a large restaurant chain sent an email to colleagues celebrating rising gas prices and inflation as good for business. His thinking was rising prices would force more people into the workforce, allowing the company to hire employees at a lower wage.

2. **Clueless comments:** No business leader in their right mind would intentionally insult potential customers, employees, or investors. But often, when asked to weigh in on an issue— especially in an internal event—leaders relax their guard, eschew formal briefings from communications, and just speak off the cuff. While that can be an authenticity bonus, there's risk in riffing when you're in a leadership position. Sans specific talking points, many leaders are subject to availability bias, relying on information that is most readily available, rather than that which is necessarily most representative.[57] We mentioned an example of this in Chapter Two. In a Zoom meeting,

[55] "APA Dictionary of Psychology." American Psychological Association Accessed March 21, 2022. https://dictionary.apa.org/confirmation-bias.

[56] Graves, Stephen R. "Are You a Tone-Deaf Leader?" Dr. Stephen R. Graves. n.d. https://stephenrgraves.com/articles/read/dont-be-a-tone-deaf-leader/.

[57] "Availability Bias." Catalog of Bias. n.d. https://catalogofbias.org/biases/availability-bias/.

the CEO of one of the largest banks in the U.S. exasperated Black employees when he reiterated that the bank had trouble reaching diversity goals because there were not enough qualified "minority" candidates.

3. **Dismissive remarks:** No matter where leaders start, by the time they reach senior level in most organizations, there's an inevitable disconnect. For top leaders in the largest organizations, that disconnect can be significant. According to the Economic Policy Institute, since 1978, CEO pay has skyrocketed 1,322%, and in 2020, CEOs were paid 351 times as much as a typical worker.[58] Socially, economically, and professionally, they're just in a whole different class, part of an entirely different ingroup. Even the most engaged and empathetic leaders may naturally fall prey to ingroup/outgroup bias, feeling more empathy for those who are in their group and less for those who aren't.

4. **The silent treatment:** According to the 2022 Edelman Trust Barometer, distrust is the default now; nearly six in 10 respondents said they distrust something until they see evidence it is trustworthy.[59] It's the spurious-until-proven-sincere principle. However, if people trust any institution, they trust business—more than NGOs, government, and media. Seventy-seven percent of people trust their employer most. However, most people think business is slacking on societal issues, especially climate change and economic inequality. It's a strong case for why leaders cannot afford to stay silent on issues that matter to their stakeholders and align with their organizational mission.

[58] Mishel, L., & Kandra, J. "CEO pay has skyrocketed 1,322% since 1978: CEOS were paid 351 times as much as a typical worker in 2020." Economic Policy Institute. Accessed March 19, 2022. https://www.epi.org/publication/ceo-pay-in-2020/.

[59] "2022 Edelman Trust Barometer." Edelman. https://www.edelman.com/sites/g/files/aatuss191/files/2022-01/2022%20Edelman%20Trust%20Barometer%20FINAL_Jan25.pdf.

Yet, in an increasingly polarized, damned-if-you-do-damned-if-you-don't world, it's easy to understand why leaders might fall prey to status-quo biases, keeping things as they are, and loss aversion, or going to great lengths to avoid a negative outcome—even if it's possible that the outcome could be positive.[60] That's exactly what happened when the CEO of Disney™ initially decided to stay quiet about Florida's "Don't Say Gay" bill.

Leaders don't generally set out to say something that's flat-out wrong. Rather, it's either insensitive, inadequate, or incompatible with the mission. It can be the result of cluelessness or ignorance. Whatever the intent, the impact of what leaders say means leaders can't afford to make mistakes.

LAUNCHING LEGACIES

What many leaders know is that communication misspeaks have implications beyond the current media moment; they can tarnish a professional legacy.

Leaving a legacy is important to leaders. In its recent Global Human Capital Trends report, Deloitte found that when CEOs were asked to rate their most important measure of success, the number one issue they cited was "impact on society, including income inequality, diversity, and the environment."[61]

Launching that legacy is important to everyone else too. Sixty percent of employees want their CEO to speak out, shape conversation, and drive policy on key societal issues such as job availability and the

---

[60] "APA Dictionary of Psychology." American Psychological Association. Accessed March 21, 2022. https://dictionary.apa.org/behavioral-economics.

[61] *Leading the Social Enterprise: Reinvent with a Human Focus: 2019 Deloitte Global Human Capital Trends.* Deloitte. https://www2.deloitte.com/content/dam/insights/us/articles/5136_HC-Trends-2019/DI_HC-Trends-2019.pdf.

economy, wage inequity, technology and automation, and global warming and climate change. And 80% of the general population wants personal visibility from CEOs when discussing public policy with external stakeholders or describing what their companies are doing to benefit society.

Leadership legacies start with the leader's vision. Think about what a vision is, actually. It's the aspiration and articulation of the world one wants to see and a guiding beacon that directs internal decision-making; it's the *why*. Visions—at least the ones that drive successful organizations—transcend the terrestrial. They go beyond returning value to shareholders and making money. They are transformational rather than transactional. They have DEPTH. And that's where communicators can help.

THE COMMUNICATOR'S ROLE IN HELPING LEADERS LEAD

How do we help leaders shape and share those visions? The DEPTH Model can help. It provides a less threatening way to help leaders understand why they say legacy-limiting stupid sh*t and discover more affirming ways to develop legacy-launching smart sh*t. It's the equal and opposite reaction to the biases that lead to misspeak.

Shaping Vision with DEPTH

Let's start by examining which DEPTH principle each type of misspeak violates and how.

1. **Insensitive statements** are statements that are misinformed and misaligned with their mission and vision. Because they result from not knowing what's going on, they typically violate the EDUCATED principle. When it's a matter of losing sight of the audience, they go against the TAILORED principal as well. It happens; leaders are busy. Help them.

2. Clueless comments result from not knowing what's happening in the moment and, sometimes, being unaware of what others—even the leader themselves—have said previously. Being EDUCATED in communications limits misspeaks; being HABITUAL can make saying the right thing automatic.

3. Dismissive remarks, like insensitive statements and clueless comments, stem from just not knowing, not being EDUCATED. But they also happen when leaders lack or lose sight of the vision when they aren't PURPOSEFUL.

4. The silent treatment happens when leaders fail to see the real problem and how it's connected to the company mission, in violation of the DELIBERATE and PURPOSEFUL principles.

So, what can you do about these misspeaks? Use The DEPTH Model to stay ahead of the problem by building a reference library:

▸ *Create a list of key topics around DEI and social justice.* These should be topics that your leaders are best able to speak about based on who they are and what your company does, so analyze them with The DEPTH Model. The topics should be issues that you know will come up; make sure you know or develop your organization's position on them. Update this list by keeping an eye on current events, what others in your industry are saying, and the issues your leaders have tackled previously. Doing this step also helps build the habit muscle and, once implemented, builds the trail of proof points.

▸ *Turn the list into one-page briefs.* Each brief should include what the issue is, two to three sentences defining or describing it; why it's important; current dialogue on it, including opposing views on it; why your organization is making a statement about it; what your organization is doing about it; and links to the most current information you can find about it. Use The DEPTH

Model's *CONSIDER* questions to shape your position, and the *CLARIFY* statements to articulate that position. The format should be standardized for easy comprehension.

▸ Save the library on a shared drive that leaders can access. Include a field, "Updated on:" with a date, and review the briefs regularly, especially the ones you know leaders will need to respond to.

Proactively, make it a policy to include the most critical briefs in whatever regular information process your leaders use. If they have weekend "folders," start including briefs. Monday morning calendar reviews? Issue a brief. Make the briefs part of their routine to keep the issues top of mind.

Reactively, when you have to clean up a communications mess, have the briefs ready and make sure they are accessible to leaders and their staff. Use them to shape whatever response is necessary. And speaking of responses … How do you help a leader say sorry?

SAYING SORRY WITH DEPTH

As children, most of us are taught to apologize when we make a mistake or say something we shouldn't. As adults and leaders, apologies—just like statements—carry a lot of weight. As communicators, it's our job to help our companies and leaders shoulder that weight.

A leader's apology can have political or financial implications for a company. It's never just for themselves; a leader's apology stands for the entire organization, from the employees to the board. As Barbara Kellerman, Founding Executive Director and (now) Fellow at the Harvard Kennedy School's Center for Public Leadership, states, "A leader's apology is a performance in which every expression matters, and every word becomes part of the public record."[62]

---

[62] Kellerman, Barbara. "When Should a Leader Apologize-and When Not?" Harvard Business Review. n.d. https://hbr.org/2006/04/when-should-a-leader-apologize-and-when-not.

There are four essential steps to a public apology:

1. Admit the mistake or misspeak
2. Accept responsibility
3. Acknowledge concern
4. Address with action

While these elements are present in any good apology, they are especially crucial if the misspeak concerns a social justice or DEI issue, both of which are sensitive by their very nature. When a product fails, it can be recalled, replaced and, if done correctly, the company can bounce back. The Tylenol® recall of 1982 is the textbook example of a company apologizing for a product problem. When someone laced bottles of Tylenol with cyanide and seven people died, Tylenol makers Johnson & Johnson went through all the steps in exactly the right way, and bounced back better than ever.

But a leader's misspeak mea culpa is a little harder to correct. For one thing, they usually can't hide behind the company; they generally must speak for themselves, personally. They must, in accepting responsibility and acknowledging concern, validate the seemingly subjective grievances of a particular group, the validity of which they may or may not believe in, personally or politically. And they must ameliorate for a personal misspeak with a company action that stakeholders may neither agree with nor feel obligated to follow through on.

As the following chart shows, The DEPTH Model serves as an objective framework for shaping an apology when the issue is more subjective.

The DEPTH Model™ serves as an objective framework for shaping an apology when the issue is more subjective.

			Accurately **decide on positioning**
ADMIT the mistake or misspeak	**DELIBERATE**	Clearly **define the problem** — the true nature of the misspeak and the offense	Accurately **decide on positioning**
ACCEPT responsibility	**EDUCATED**	**Explore the history and context** of the issue **Engage other perspectives**, especially the perspectives of those most affected	**Expand the conversation** by identifying who was harmed and acknowledging the existence of the systemic inequities that shape such responses
ACKNOWLEDGE concern	**PURPOSEFUL**	**Position the purpose** of the apology in relation to the company's values	**Promote the purpose** by explaining how the misspeak deviated from it
ADDRESS with action	**TAILORED**	**Take stock of capabilities** to determine if what you're promising is something you can actually do	**Tailor your message** to be actionable rather than aspirational
	HABITUAL	**Hone your commitment** to show how the action you're taking now is — or will be — part of an ongoing commitment	**Hold the line** going forward and defend the response if the issue resurfaces

The Conscious Communicator
The first art of not saying stupid sh*t

©

For a downloadable copy of this graphic, please visit https://theconsciouscommunicator.com/

KEY TAKEAWAYS

1. Leaders' words go far and dig deep, affecting those they lead, reflecting on the brands they represent, and showing us who they are—the first time.

2. Communicators cannot control what a leader says in the moment, but they can use The DEPTH Model proactively and reactively to minimize misspeaks or mitigate their damage.

3. Conscious communicators help leaders choose their words consciously to support the company's mission and to avoid saying stupid sh*t.

The Business of Business Is People: How Deeply Does Your CEO Understand? How Deeply Do You?

by David Murray

As a member of a corporate board, I'd be inclined to forgive a CEO who still struggled, even after the events of 2020 and 2021, to see the dramatic expansion of the chief executive's role into the realm of social responsibility.

Inclined to forgive the CEO—as I gently show them to the door.

Why inclined to forgive?

CEOs did not attend business school (or economics school or engineering school) in order to run social institutions. In their hard-driving early career years, their laser focus did not allow for a lot of contemplation of social issues, let alone the acquisition of cultural literacy. Precisely at what point on the hellbent climb of a CEO did we expect such people to develop a coherent and deeply felt personal philosophy on society's ills, and the role business could play in easing them? And *as* CEO, it's hard enough to make quarterly earnings *without* seeing oneself as a public intellectual and a moral leader.

Why show the door?

Because "thought leader," which was until recently the laudatory term for any CEO who took the time to pay public lip service to ideas beyond the immediate financial ken of the corporation, is now table stakes for any corporate leader who wants to survive, let alone thrive, in these redefined times. Over the last few years—in America, I actually trace this to the hyperpolarizing election of Donald Trump as U.S. president—people have been turning to CEOs for leadership, by default. The very economic self-interest that once made CEOs' views suspect to thinking people, now makes their views reliable, relatively speaking—as their self-interest includes a stable, at least moderately healthy society. And that compels CEOs to listen to, acknowledge, and satisfy angry or injured employees, customers, activist investors, and other powerful influencers who hold great sway on their permission to operate.

Such groups confront corporate CEOs at the most inconvenient times, often in impolite styles and with demands for more than words in return. Responding in the right tone and working with them with real substance is possible only for the CEO who has previously and continuously demonstrated an authentic and independent interest in social issues. Audiences can hear (and taste and smell and feel) the difference between, "I'm a corporate bean counter making this statement on another goddamn 'social issue' so I can get back to work," and, "I am always thinking, and have long been talking, about how our business interacts with the most difficult social issues of our time. In fact, what you're asking for dovetails very much with what we've been working on for several years …"

CEO watchers can easily identify examples of the former type, and also examples of the latter. Five years from now, the latter corporate leader will be the only kind left standing, the only kind who felt the job was worth the hassle, because they didn't see roiling social demands placed upon them as a "hassle" in the first place. They saw their CEO role as an incredible opportunity to use the vast economic and cultural influence of a modern corporation to make meaningful change in the world in which they operate.

"The business of business is business," Milton Friedman famously said. Milton Friedman, who is famously dead.

Obviously, modern corporate leaders *do* have terribly difficult, endlessly political jobs—that still *do* require them to make quarterly earnings. They need help in developing and articulating their ideas, in balancing conflicting demands and in focusing their energies and communications where they can do the most good. For that help, they must turn to communication professionals and other deeply culturally literate advisors—who must, themselves, believe fundamentally in the ability of corporate leaders to use their powers for good. Cynical or narrow-minded communicators will go the way of Milton Friedman, too.

If corporations are going to help make a kinder, warmer society—rather than a meaner, colder one—CEOs and their advisors both must drive themselves toward the psychically dangerous integration of their work with their intellect, their morality, their whole humanity.

It's a lot to ask. It's also the least, in exchange for corporate salaries and creature comforts afforded by so many to so few, that corporate leaders can do.

Biography

David Murray (he/him) is founder and executive director of the Professional Speechwriters Association and the Executive Communication Council. He's the author of the communicator's manifesto, An Effort to Understand: Hearing One Another (and Ourselves) in a Nation Cracked in Half *(Disruption Books, 2021).*

> *Stakeholder: Anyone with an opinion and a social media account.*

CHAPTER 10

WHAT'S AT STAKE FOR STAKEHOLDERS

*Regardless of how complicated the problems might appear,
it is possible to work through them and find solutions that are
mutually satisfactory to every stakeholder in the problem ...
most of our problems on this earth are created by us
and therefore we have the capacity and the obligation
to unmake them.*

**—Hizkias Assefa, conflict mediator
and professor of conflict studies**

The stakes are high when managing stakeholders. In DEI and social justice communications, they're stratospheric. With highly divergent opinions of highly provocative issues, finding common ground is no easy task. Conscious communicators manage stakeholders by aligning their disparate interests with organizational vision.

STAKEHOLDERS DEFINED

If the evolution of the definition of *stakeholder* were a multiple-choice quiz, it would look something like this (which/that grammar errors notwithstanding):

A) 1963: "Groups without whose support the organization would cease to exist"[63]

B) 1967: "Groups which make a difference"[64]

C) 1968: "Groups which depend on the company for the realization of their personal goals and on whom the company is dependent"[65]

D) 1993: Groups who "benefit from or are harmed by, and whose rights are violated or respected by, corporate actions"[66]

E) 2022: All of the above

In a 2013 interview, Jerry Greenfield, co-founder and namesake of Ben & Jerry's™ said, "Ben & Jerry's was based on values, and we try to operate a business that not just sells ice cream but partners with all our stakeholders—whether that's suppliers or customers—to bring about a more sustainable world."[67] They aren't perfect, but there is more thoughtfulness in what they say and do than many organizations. In 2019, the Business Roundtable put stakeholders at the center of

---

[63] 1963 Stanford Research Institute Internal Memo, cited in Freeman RE, Reed DL. *Stockholders and Stakeholders: A New Perspective on Corporate Governance.* California Management Review. 1983;25(3):88–106.

[64] Thompson, J. D. *Organizations in action: Social science bases of administrative theory.* McGraw-Hill, 1967.

[65] Rhenman, Eric. "Industrial democracy and industrial management. A critical essay on the possible meanings and implications of industrial democracy." 1968.

[66] Evan, W., & Freeman, R. E. In T. Beauchamp, & N. Bowie (Eds.), *Ethical Theory and Practice* (pp. 75–84). Englewoods Cliffs, N.J.: Prentice Hall. 1993.

[67] Jenkin, Matthew. "Ice-Cream Icon Jerry Greenfield Shares His Top Tips for Business Startups." The Guardian.

things, redefining the very purpose of a corporation. When it comes to DEI and social justice communications, meeting stakeholder expectations is a high-stakes endeavor.

Business Roundtable's Statement on the Purpose of a Corporation[68]

Americans deserve an economy that allows each person to succeed through hard work and creativity and to lead a life of meaning and dignity. We believe the free-market system is the best means of generating good jobs, a strong and sustainable economy, innovation, a healthy environment, and economic opportunity for all.

Businesses play a vital role in the economy by creating jobs, fostering innovation, and providing essential goods and services. Businesses make and sell consumer products; manufacture equipment and vehicles; support the national defense; grow and produce food; provide health care; generate and deliver energy; and offer financial, communications, and other services that underpin economic growth.

While each of our individual companies serves its own corporate purpose, we share a fundamental commitment to all of our stakeholders. We commit to:

- ► Delivering value to our customers. We will further the tradition of American companies leading the way in meeting or exceeding customer expectations.

- ► Investing in our employees. This starts with compensating them fairly and providing important benefits. It also includes supporting them through training and education that helps develop new skills for a rapidly changing world. We foster diversity and inclusion, dignity, and respect.

[68] "Business Roundtable Redefines the Purpose of a Corporation to Promote 'an Economy That Serves All Americans.'" Businessroundtable.org.

- Dealing fairly and ethically with our suppliers. We are dedicated to serving as good partners to the other companies, large and small, that help us meet our missions.

- Supporting the communities in which we work. We respect the people in our communities and protect the environment by embracing sustainable practices across our businesses.

- Generating long-term value for shareholders, who provide the capital that allows companies to invest, grow, and innovate. We are committed to transparency and effective engagement with shareholders.

Each of our stakeholders is essential. We commit to deliver value to all of them, for the future success of our companies, our communities, and our country.

THE HIGH STAKES OF STAKEHOLDER MANAGEMENT

Once upon a time, companies stayed out of social issues. Once upon a time, DEI wasn't even an issue spoken about in the workplace. Such were the times in which R. Edward Freeman, the father of stakeholder theory, explained that the success of a business rests on creating value for the people with the money, aligning their disparate interests, and making sure they go in the same direction.[69]

But times have changed. Now, for all the reasons we've discussed, companies are engaged in more than just returning value to shareholders. Companies now, whether they like it or not, are being called on to step up and speak out.

In DEI and social justice communications, where the focus is on subjective values (plural) rather than objective values, aligning

---

[69] Freeman, Edward. "Stakeholder Theory—Edward Freeman." Stakeholdermap.com. 2010.

stakeholder interests can be like the proverbial herding of cats. Trying to do it in the age of influencers, always-on and potentially viral media, is exponentially more difficult. It's no longer just about the people with money; it's about anyone willing to take a stand. So, perhaps it's time for another definition: a stakeholder can be anyone with an opinion and a social media account.

WHO MATTERS MOST?

Traditionally, stakeholders were divided into two camps: primary and secondary. Primary stakeholders are the people and groups with economic interest and interaction, such as employees, customers, suppliers, and stockholders. Secondary stakeholders are usually external, such as communities, the media, activists, and the general public. They are not involved in economic exchange, but they are able to affect or be affected by the organization.

There's a longstanding debate about which stakeholders matter most: shareholders, customers, or employees. However, the triple whammy of a pandemic, social upheaval, and economic unrest has turned academicians' intellectual argument into conscious communicators' biggest challenge.

How do you choose a direction in which to align all those interests? How do you decide what to say to whom? Whose interests do you prioritize? The answers may not be simple, but they're straightforward.

THE COMMUNICATOR'S ROLE
IN MANAGING STAKEHOLDERS

Three rules can help communicators deal with what's at stake when dealing with stakeholders:

1. **Follow the vision.** For conscious communicators, stakeholders are myriad and stakeholder primacy is relative. Communications accountability is top-down and bottom-up;

internal and external; departmentally and organizationally scoped. Given the sensitive, often polarizing nature of DEI and social justice communications, communicators need a single source of truth, a North Star towards which to steer. Follow the vision.

The vision is a single thing that all stakeholders can agree on. It's a rallying point. It's a superordinate goal: something that takes precedence over other, more conditional goals; something attainable only if the two or more groups pool their skills, efforts, and resources and work together to achieve it.[70]

A clearly stated vision—aspiration made actionable by the organization's core capabilities—is something most of your stakeholders can embrace. It's why they chose to be stakeholders in the first place.

2. **Focus on those most affected.** DEI and social justice communications, by their very nature, center fairness and equity—for somebody. If the issue aligns with the organization's vision and if the organization chooses to engage, the primary stakeholder should be the group most affected. In many cases, that's the group most harmed. In most cases, it probably will be clear which group that is.

3. **Communicate with DEPTH.** If it's not clear who the most affected stakeholders are, it's time to get in DEPTH. The DEPTH Model can streamline the thought process. The Stakeholder Alignment Tool uses DEPTH to prioritize action based on who the stakeholder is and what their in-the-moment point of pain may be.

---

[70] "APA Dictionary of Psychology." American Psychological Association. Accessed March 21, 2022. https://dictionary.apa.org/superordinate-goal.

THE STAKEHOLDER ALIGNMENT TOOL

DEI and social justice issues bring out both the best and worst in stakeholders. The Stakeholder Alignment Tool uses The DEPTH Model to help you communicate consciously to the people who matter most.

While stakeholders and organizations will differ, the Stakeholder Alignment Tool looks at some common concerns of common audiences. The tool suggests which DEPTH pillar you should work to address depending on what the concern is and why that pillar is most important. You can easily add or adjust elements as needed.

STAKEHOLDER ALIGNMENT TOOL

	CONCERN		FOCUS
The Communications Team	Making clear where leadership stands on an issue	DELIBERATE	Define the problem
	Proving value to leadership	EDUCATED	Position communications as Subject Matter Experts
	Mitigating employee blowback	HABITUAL	Minimize blowback
The C-Suite	Improving employee engagement	PURPOSEFUL	Publicize the purpose
	Positioning the brand competitively	TAILORED	Connect to core competencies
	Dealing with the Board		Align with stakeholders
DEI and HR Leadership	Attracting & retaining diverse talent	PURPOSEFUL	Align with vision & mission
	Creating an inclusive culture	HABITUAL	Sustain characteristic messages
	Delivering on DEI goals	DELIBERATE	Articulate problems & solutions
Customers and Prospects	Knowing where the company stands	DELIBERATE	Decide on position
	Knowing what the company can do	TAILORED	Connect to core competencies
	Believing company keeps its promises	HABITUAL	Hone your commitment
Employees	Knowing where leadership stands	DELIBERATE	Decide on position
	Knowing what the company stands for	PURPOSEFUL	Align with vision & mission
	Believing company keeps its promises	HABITUAL	Communicate consistently

The Conscious Communicator
The Fine Art of Not Saying Stupid Sh*t

For a downloadable copy of this graphic, please visit https://theconsciouscommunicator.com/

KEY TAKEAWAYS

1. Stakeholders now expect companies and their leaders to take a stand on DEI and social justice issues.

2. In the age of social media, a stakeholder can be anyone with an opinion and a social media account.

3. Conscious communicators manage stakeholders by aligning their disparate interests with organizational vision.

The High Stakes of Dealing with DEI Stakeholders

by Charlene Thomas

In the DEI space, communications has two goals: transparency and clarity. And they are neither mutually exclusive nor different. For Chief Human Resource Officers (CHROs) and Chief Diversity Officer/Chief Diversity and Inclusion Officers (CDIOs), the difference lies in how you define the "e:" equity.

For the CHRO, both dimensions of equity—fairness and finances—are important. CHROs typically are members of the board compensation committee, the management liaison on executive compensation issues. CHROs also are the board's go-to on talent-related issues, fielding questions around what the organization is doing to recruit, retain, recognize, and reward critical talent. When DEI is a metric used to determine executive compensation—as it increasingly is—what executives *receive* in equity can be determined by what the company *does* to advance equity. Namely, fairness can drive finances.

CHROs have an internal responsibility to employees because DEI is the right thing to do, but they're also accountable in terms of governance and external, public-facing positioning. When leaders lose financial equity because the company has not advanced people's equity, their bank accounts aren't the only thing that takes a hit. Salaries and bonuses of (at least) the top five highest-paid executives are listed in the proxy for the world to see. Investors and shareholders are two critical stakeholders that definitely look. For CHROs, DEI communications is about having a consistent, universal, transparent approach that shapes how key stakeholders—the board of directors, external shareholders, internal executives, and the general public—view the company and its equity success or failure.

For CDIOs, however, DEI communications focus more on the culture, the employee experience. They're about sustaining employee engagement by showing how the company is walking its DEI talk. But that doesn't mean metrics don't matter. Like the CHRO, the CDIO is concerned about the company hitting its DEI numbers because they are a measure of whether or not the company is meeting stated aspirational goals. When communicated well, those numbers also can ensure higher Net Promoter Scores, the measure of loyalty to a company, and likelihood to recommend it to others. CDIOs also look to DEI communications to help them create and steer policy to ensure more equity and to secure buy-in. A CDIO's programs and protocols are in the hands of their peers. They must, through good DEI communications, influence and engage those responsible for the employee experience.

Because they have challenging stakeholders, CHROs and CDIOs are challenging stakeholders to have. In addition, for every measure of DEI communications enthusiasm, there's an equal measure of DEI communications resistance. Boards, directors, senior leaders—in DEI, everyone wants to share representation hits, but no one wants to talk about misses. Even communicating DEI aspirational goals can be difficult because communicability leads to accountability, and for all the aforementioned reasons, that can be a scary proposition. In DEI communications, CDIOs focus internally to ensure positive external perceptions; CHROs leverage potentially negative external perceptions to drive internal accountability.

However, while leaders may be the DEI communicator's primary stakeholder, they are far from the predominant one. That distinction goes to employees.

There is an immediate flashpoint with employees around DEI messaging. It generally comes in two veins: pay equity and representation of underrepresented groups. If the company makes or has made promises or set goals, but there's no movement in middle management levels, employees will question the organization's commitment to equity. Often valid reasons—other priorities, business imperatives, best intentions—matter little to employees seeking insight about who gets promoted and paid. DEI communicators often find themselves torn between employees' need for transparency around impact and leadership's concern about expediency of intent.

So, what makes for good DEI communications? It must be concise. It must clearly address pain points. It can't employ a lot of language that says nothing. DEI communications must address issues—positive or negative—truthfully, honestly, concisely, leaving no room for subjective interpretations of what the organization or leader intended, what they hoped to portray. In some types of communication, plucking the good story from the bad situation is a great skill. Not in DEI. DEI communications asks and answers the questions, "What are we solving for and how are we going to solve it?" Good DEI communications helps its stakeholders retain and maintain credibility with their stakeholders.

What makes for a good DEI communicator? I believe effective DEI communicators possess lived or learned personal experience of DEI challenges. They are representative of the stories they're trying to tell; not consumed with the language used to communicate, but focused on the benefit of what's being communicated, understanding the best opportunity to reach optimal engagement, truth, and transparency. DEI communicators don't have to be born with that kind of insight, but they must work diligently and consistently to secure and sustain it. The stakes are high in DEI; dealing with its stakeholders is not for the faint of heart.

Biography

Charlene Thomas (she/her) serves as Executive Vice President (EVP) and Chief Diversity, Equity, and Inclusion Officer (CDIO) for UPS and is a member of the company's Executive Leadership Team. In her previous role of Chief Human Resources Officer, she guided UPS's transformation and HR initiatives to optimize the talent, leadership, and culture for the company's more than 528,000 employees worldwide.

CHAPTER 11

DIFFERENCE DIALOGUE

It is not our differences that divide us.
It is our inability to recognize, accept,
and celebrate those differences.

—Audre Lorde, American writer, feminist,
womanist, librarian, and civil rights activist

Talking about difference is difficult. We come at it from varying angles and perspectives using diverse languages. Difference dialogue is disruptive because it involves revealing truths, righting wrongs, and requiring accountability. But talking about difference is doable if we collaborate realistically, engage authentically, and support intentionally.

WHAT IS DIFFERENCE DIALOGUE?

Difference dialogue is being able to talk freely about our differences without feeling intimidated and without being scared of offending someone or hurting someone's feelings—and it's really important for communicators working in the DEI and social justice space. Indeed, difference dialogue is critical in all professional spaces because it's one of the most important keys to unlocking the power of diversity.

There are three things to know about difference dialogue: First, difference dialogue is difficult. There are many issues, impediments, and ideologies that make it extremely hard to acknowledge and talk about difference in the workplace.

Second, difference dialogue is disruptive. The silence of the status quo is always easier. However, talking about difference is one of the most powerful ways to build the culture of inclusion necessary for conscious communication. It's the only way to ensure your communications are EDUCATED. Not talking about difference is a missed opportunity for communicators to make a real difference.

But, third, difference dialogue is doable, especially now. Social justice and inequity once were intellectual and moral discussions for the classroom, pulpit, or dinner table. However, as attorney Valerie Kennedy wrote recently, "The subject of race is having a Cinderella moment in the American spotlight."[71] Race, gender orientation, ability—for a moment at least, the unspoken ban on speaking openly about differences in the corporate sector has been lifted. So it is, too, with just about every issue that has an element of inequity or injustice. So, why is it so hard to talk about this stuff at work? And what can make it easier?

BIAS, INCLUSION, AND ALLYSHIP

Even the most open-minded of us struggle to deal with and talk about inequity, injustice, and fairness, which is, in the end, what most DEI and social justice issues boil down to. Whether we are in the majority or minority, the privileged or marginalized position, these topics just aren't

[71] Kennedy, V. "Does corporate diversity and inclusion enable systemic racism?" Medium. Accessed December 31, 2021.

easy to face. However, as communicators, we no longer have a choice about doing so. It's not personal; it's professional. But first, we have to tackle bias—our own and that of everyone else. Because we have both conscious and unconscious biases at play, difference dialogue can be challenging.

The first step in dealing with cognitive biases is to acknowledge they exist. We all have them, and they affect our behavior and decisions. Once we accept that, we can determine when and how they are operating. One way to do this is by asking ourselves why we aren't really listening to—as evidenced by not acting on or disputing—the perspectives of people who differ from us or why we're making assumptions about them that have no basis in our actual experience. "Women are more nurturing." "Black people are cool." "Latinos are fiery." "Asians are smart." Each of these statements could have some truth behind them, but do we know for sure that these things are *universally* true? Are they true for every person in our friend group or our team who is a member of the group? Doubtful. Accepting our biases is huge—but it's not enough.

Once we accept bias, the next step is to become intentionally inclusive. We must start asking for and listening to other perspectives, and then acting on what we hear to change what we say or how we proceed. Harvard Business School colleagues Robin Ely and David A. Thomas call this the Learning-and-Effectiveness Paradigm: leveraging difference by admitting that it exists, understanding what it means, and then applying it to reimagine what and how we create.[72]

The next step is allyship. A step beyond inclusion, allyship is when someone uses the privilege they have to level the playing field for members of a specific group of people who lack that privilege. And just as we must acknowledge our biases, we must recognize our privilege. Privilege is simply having an advantage that others don't have in a given

---

[72] Ely, Robin and Thomas, David A. *Getting Serious About Diversity: Enough Already with the Business Case.* Harvard Business Review 98, no. 6 (November–December 2020).

situation. This means anyone could have privilege depending on the situation. Sure, some groups have that advantage most of the time, but that could change if the situation changes. Being an ally is about speaking up when someone is being silenced.

Team interactions provide the most opportunity to be an ally and advance difference dialogue. As we become more skilled at allyship, we can become accomplices; putting our own privilege at risk to dismantle performative systems and disrupt the -isms that perpetuate the status quo. From accomplices, we can become advocates, deploying a range of strategies and tactics to move people to action. And moving people to action is what communication is all about.

DIFFERENCE DIALOGUE AT VARYING LEVELS

In teams, the discussion often centers on inclusion, respect, and privilege. Whose voices are heard? Whose opinions and ideas are included? Who is even in the room?

Talking about sensitive issues isn't hard just for those in the majority/privileged position. For those in marginalized positions, it takes energy to talk about the things that frustrate and traumatize them. So, when we're asking those most harmed to provide input, understand that providing it is cathartic only once or twice. After that, especially if that input is ignored, it's just more trauma. But what do we do when the dialogue needs to happen with people we report up to?

When we see potentially biased, discriminatory, or uninformed comments coming from people higher on the org chart, it feels risky to confront them. Whether or not we do depends on several factors, none of which is written in stone or definitive for a particular circumstance. When we're dealing with our superiors, we may not be able to have an actual conversation.

When having difference dialogue with your teammates:

1. Make sure you've already done some homework of your own on whatever the issue is that prompts the need for difference dialogue. Not just the basic details, but through a DEI LENS , thinking about how the person with whom you're going to engage might think differently about whatever it is you're going to engage on. Don't ask stupid sh*t.

2. If something happens and you need to develop a response, ask and then listen to someone who is most knowledgeable or most harmed. As hard as it may be, keep your mouth shut and your ears open. Chances are your questions, even the ones it's best not to ask, will be answered before you even have to ask them. And when it is time to engage, don't tell your side of the story unless there is, legitimately, another side to the story and unless you, legitimately, are the person to tell it. If that's the case, do so without de-legitimizing, dismissing or dissing the person you're talking to. Believe others' lived experience—the first time.

3. Seek diverse perspectives on things other than the obvious issues. If your organization was going to take a stand on Florida's "Don't Say Gay" bill, then of course you'd ask a member of the LGBTQ+ community. But what if your organization was developing a statement about housing discrimination? Chances are, there is a different perspective there. Don't tokenize—leverage.

When talking to your superiors, assess the situation and respond accordingly:

1. If there's going to be backlash, push the difference dialogue up the org chart. This is true in any case, but especially true when external audiences are concerned. Not that internal audiences should be ignored; they just have a vested interest in being more tolerant, at least for a while. Hopefully, the leader who

needs to have this dialogue will appreciate your courage in speaking up. But before you do, validate what you are going to say. If there's written support you can provide, do it.

For example, if someone on the executive team constantly uses the term "Latinx," find articles or studies that support your point about why many Latinos don't care for or use that term. Even if you happen to be the DEI communications expert on the issue—objectivity makes difference dialogue easier. It also makes it easier for you to step back if the leader is less than interested in hearing others' opinions. Unfortunately, this sometimes is the case. If you can, ask and alert someone who is closer to the person making the statement. For example, if it's the CEO, alert the highest-ranking person in the communications team to the issue and explain the potential blowback. If that person doesn't say anything, at least you've done your job.

2. If the leader is just clueless, pick your battles. As a communications person, you often see and hear more from leaders than many others in a company. And that means you're privy to them saying the quiet stuff out loud. Maybe it will never blow up. Maybe the person doesn't even mean the things they say. But impact overshadows intent. Bias is real and privilege blinds us; your greatest strength is in helping leaders find and eliminate their weak spots.

For communicators, stakeholders are an important constituency, in addition to peers and superiors, for two reasons. First, because stakeholders are a challenge. We are the ones who must speak to them, which means navigating the many ways people view difference, as a valuable resource or a looming threat. Second, because stakeholders are an opportunity. We also are the ones who can create the connections between the differing views of difference. When we engage stakeholders, our messages go farther. By creating shared, superordinate goals, conscious communicators give DEI and social justice communications greater weight, higher reach—depth.

THE COMMUNICATOR'S ROLE
IN DRIVING DIFFERENCE DIALOGUE

The DEPTH Model both encourages and requires difference dialogue at several points. For EDUCATED communications, exploring history and engaging other perspectives allows you to not only avoid saying stupid sh*t, but also expand the conversation in nuanced ways. Being DELIBERATE calls for defining the problem your communications are trying to solve, a process made easier, faster, and more accurate with diverse input. If your company claims diversity and inclusion as part of its vision, PURPOSEFUL communications would demand that the diversity be leveraged via inclusion. Finally, difference dialogue can help you uncover core capabilities to tell your story for TAILORED communications; making difference dialogue HABITUAL makes that insight a sustainable process.

Difference dialogue allows us to unleash the power of diversity. Difference dialogue gives us a framework for allyship. Difference dialogue is the language of change.

KEY TAKEAWAYS

1. Difference dialogue, talking freely about differences, is critical for DEI and social justice communicators.

2. Difference dialogue is difficult and disruptive, but it is also doable.

3. Conscious communications in the DEI and social justice space calls for difference dialogue to find and leverage diverse perspectives.

From Mythology to Possibility

by Dr. Jennifer A. Richeson

There's a thin line between reality and mythology. Most of us regularly cross that line, especially when discussing our differences. But communicators—more than most—must know which side they're on.

Communicators should base their work in truth, and most believe they do. However, belief bias, which the American Psychological Association (APA) defines as "the tendency to be influenced by one's knowledge about the world in evaluating conclusions and to accept them as true because they are believable rather than because they are logically valid," can lead them to confuse opinion with fact, to accept things as objectively true without digging deeper.[73] One thing most of us believe—despite logical validity—is the mythology of racial progress. And as hard as it is to communicate across differences, it's even harder when our perceptions become our reality.

Mythology vs. Reality

The mythology of racial progress is that it can and does happen automatically, naturally, and on its own; that we're steadily, automatically, readily making progress toward greater racial equality.

For many, that's "evidenced" by the civil rights movement and the legislation that came from it. For some, it's the election of Barack Obama as the first Black president of the United States.

---

[73] "APA Dictionary of Psychology." American Psychological Association. Accessed August 6, 2022. https://dictionary.apa.org/belief-bias.

156

For others, it's the very clear, very visible success of Black celebrities, athletes, politicians, and business people. These all are apparent inflection points in our progress to a predestined outcome of racial equality.

However, as much as we claim to live in a post-racial society that has advanced significantly toward equity, not much has actually changed economically, politically, and socially, and some things are swinging back. If we truly are moving toward racial equity, why are the scales still so unbalanced? This question was at the root of my research.

Research Says...

In 2019, my Yale colleague Michael W. Kraus, our students, and I, published a study comparing people's perceptions of racial economic inequality with actual data over time. The study spanned a 53-year period from 1963 to 2016. As one might suspect, study participants believed the wealth of the average Black family and that of the average white family was closer to being equal than it actually was. For 1963, they perceived Black family wealth to be just about under 50% of the average white family. It actually was only 5%. For 2016, they perceived Black wealth as almost 90% that of whites. It was about 10%. The estimates weren't just wrong, they got more wrong over time. Why? Because people assume things have gotten better and are continuing to get better.

The narrative of increasing linear, steady progress, this mythology of racial progress, distorted their perception of reality. The reality is the Black-white racial wealth gap has barely budged; it is almost as wide as it was in 1965. U.S. neighborhoods are more segregated than they were a generation ago. That wealth gap, exacerbated by racial and residential segregation, means majority school districts are far better funded than minority districts, perpetuated by and perpetuating racial inequality.

Across all of our studies, one of the most clear and consistent findings is that the extent to which people believe in a different narrative, that outcomes in life are solely dependent on one's talent, hard work, and effort, and wholly independent of structural barriers like racism or economic disadvantage—aka, the American dream—predicts how much they overestimate the current state of racial equality.

You can see this logic happening; people—including communicators—conforming their estimates to their perceptions, despite counter evidence in the world that vast racial equality still exists.

Reality and…possibility

Like most stories, this narrative has taken mythic space in our national imagination. It shapes what we see and how we perceive the actual state of racial inequality. And it patterns not only what we think about the current state of racial inequality, it also is likely to affect racial inequality in the future. Because if you believe racial progress is happening already, the logical conclusion is why do anything to move it along? Why attempt to communicate across differing perceptions? We're seeing this "logic" play out in everything from voting rights to college admissions. The mythology of racial progress can lead to assumptions that are untrue and harmful.

But does this mean there has been no racial progress? Is that what I'm saying? No, it's not. What I am suggesting is that we accept reality but perceive possibility. That when we talk and write about racial progress, we do so from a position of truth.

Even if—especially if—that truth is upsetting. Communicators have a unique ability to shape perceptions. The possibility of racial progress rests in their ability to shape perceptions based in reality. It's a big responsibility. It's an even bigger opportunity.

Biography

Dr. Jennifer A. Richeson (she/her) is an American social psychologist who studies the psychology of societal inequality. She currently is the Philip R. Allen Professor of Psychology at Yale University where she heads the Social Perception and Communication Lab, and is recognized for her work examining the psychological phenomena of cultural diversity, social group memberships, dynamics of race and racism, and interracial interactions. She also is a MacArthur Fellow, a Guggenheim fellow, and a member of the National Academy of Sciences of the United States.

*Progress isn't linear,
it's more circular.*

CHAPTER 12

OVERCOMING OBSTACLES TO DEI

"As you discover what strength you can draw from your community in this world from which it stands apart, look outward as well as inward. Build bridges instead of walls."

—Sonia Sotomayor, U.S. Supreme Court Justice

"Be hard and critical on structures, but soft on people," says john a. powell.[74] Whenever there's a disruption to the status quo, there's pushback. Anything that shifts the configuration of perceived power, meets resistance.

Communicators in some organizations are questioned about why corporate communications is getting involved in DEI. In some situations, pushback is overt: leaders prioritize other things, criticize efforts as ineffective, or reject the work without explanation.

---

[74] Powell, John A. www.news.berkeley.edu/2021/01/25/to-end-white-supremacy-attack-racist-policy-not-people/.

The pushback also can be more subtle, with excuses such as limited or non-existent resources. For example, they provide an abysmal budget that won't pay for one speaker during Pride month.

So, what is the DEI pushback about? What's going on? In Chapter one, we introduced you to Rev. Deborah L. Johnson. In her long career as a DEI consultant and trainer, Johnson has been involved in every major movement since the mid-1960s. She offers some background and lessons for us to keep in mind that help us stay committed to the work, even if we're alone in doing it at our organization:

- ▶ Progress isn't linear, it's more circular.

- ▶ We cannot expect everyone to enjoy or like progress.

- ▶ It's turned into a game of who feels empowered to silence others and stay in positions of power.

- ▶ We have to build skills in articulating why progress is a good thing, including the benefits for the people who think they are losing something.

- ▶ Be inclusive of those who are pushing back. Write them into the story.

- ▶ Do the work *with* people, not *for* people.

- ▶ Restore balance. The things we do to empower marginalized populations are the things we have to do with the dominant population that fears marginalization.

- ▶ All anyone wants is to be seen, heard, and valued.

- ▶ We don't need more othering. We don't need more people feeling marginalized and left without a chair when the music stops.

- ▶ DEI leaders and communicators aren't pulling away the chairs, but we haven't yet built a sense of trust with all of our stakeholders and audiences.

Don't wait around for or try to make everyone understand. That may never happen for some people. Most of us don't understand how a plane flies and yet we pay hundreds of dollars to go over 30,000 feet into the air and get us across the country. We will never truly understand someone else's experience and that's not the goal. We are to listen, believe, and act on bettering their experience. In bettering their experience, we will all benefit.

We can stop DEI communications pushback by leaders and skeptics by acknowledging its impact on all, writing them into the DEI narrative using The DEPTH Model, and building trust that there is a place for everyone.[75]

CHANGE THE NARRATIVE, CHANGE THE PARADIGM

Knowing that there's an undercurrent that can hinder our efforts, we can use one of our best superpowers as communicators: changing the narrative. We're really good at this when we need to be, and right now we need to be.

With every cultural shift in the last hundred years—civil rights, the Equal Rights Amendment, women's rights, LGBTQ+ rights, disability rights, and many more—an increasing number of people understand the need for historical and social context for DEI communications. As the pace of these shifts quickens, the ground is ripe for planting DEI communications from day one into our day-to-day processes. In doing so, we have to address at least three damaging paradigms from the past that keep us from moving forward.

The first paradigm is DEI communications as an afterthought; it is only done in the face of societal pressure. If this paradigm is in the way, we will never build the credibility that's possible if we actively deny the

---

[75] "Understanding the DEI Backlash." https://www.linkedin.com/pulse/understanding-dei-backlash-kim-clark.

true state of the world and basic human rights. If we want the benefits of DEI communications in our work, we must embed them into our processes from the very beginning. We don't get peaches if we plant tomatoes, no matter how hard we cross our fingers and wish. What we plant, we grow. For DEI to be an outcome, it has to be a part of what we do. If we want DEI as a result, it has to be a part of our processes.

The next unhelpful paradigm is that DEI communications is a problem to solve. Our mindset of, "Let's fix it and save the day!" doesn't work this time. Keep in mind what DEI is strategically solving for in our organization. DEI is not the problem. It's both *solution and outcome*. DEI communications helps forward our company's DEI goals by dismantling the idea that spin is good or necessary because it protects the company. This is a very old-school way of doing communications that absolutely won't work moving forward. We have to be honest, we have to be transparent, and we have to be empathetic. And that means owning the narrative without gaslighting, patronizing, or being condescending.

Shifting away from an approach that is familiar and may have worked in the past may take time, but it will be harder down the road if we don't make the necessary changes now. More established companies may believe they are too far in to create space for something new, but we have seen 100-year-old companies challenge themselves by implementing DEI communications. There is room for change when we do what we can with where we are using what's under our control. We can improve policies, review content, invest in better measurement tools, better stock footage libraries, and the list goes on.

We also hear a lot of variations on the third paradigm: "The shift is too hard." In reality, shifts are constant in business. For example, take the digital transformation. It felt unknown, expensive, and uncomfortable for some people—incorporating computers, smartphones, or virtual meetings. There was resistance, and companies that did not overcome that resistance probably did not survive.

DEI communications is the next business communication transformation. Think about how often we shift lenses in a day. We have a revenue lens, a customer acquisition and retention lens, and an employee satisfaction lens. It simply is not true to say that it is too difficult to learn the skills needed to apply a DEI LENS on our work every day.

Like any change management initiative, it requires learning new skills, bringing in people from the outside to help us learn and change behavior, and training people on the inside on systems and processes that may be new to them. We need to bring our teams along, help them see themselves in the better future, and set them up for success.

INCLUSIVE DESIGN PRINCIPLES FOR DEI COMMUNICATIONS

DEI communication is informed by something higher, whether it's a vision, a mission, or what's happening in the world. Thus, we can't treat it like something to check the box. DEI communications should be *part* of the marketing plan, but it should not be *the* marketing plan. For example, we may have a DEI communications plan as part of the overall hybrid work plan, but then we look through a DEI LENS and ask questions like: Does everyone have access to technology at home? Does everyone know how to use it? Can everybody speak the company's business language of choice (English, Spanish, Japanese, etc.)? If not, how are we supporting accessibility? Are we, for example, providing translation with social context (straightforward translation of text does not equal cultural translation—some areas may need cultural context for better understanding and inclusivity)? At the very least, are we compliant with accessibility standards in Section 508 of the Rehabilitation Act in the U.S.[76]? We no longer just assume these things once our

---

[76] Section 508 of the Rehabilitation Act in the U.S. https://www.ada.gov/508/#:~:text=Overview,and%20members%20of%20the%20public.

plan is fully integrated into all communication areas of the company. It prompts us to think about our audiences who haven't been centered in communications decision-making consistently and historically.

We can accomplish this by incorporating a communications version of Korn Ferry™'s Inclusive Design Principles. Korn Ferry,[77] a global organizational consulting firm, shares profound research covering several topics, such as how women end up with different injuries than men in car crashes, and why so many women have sweaters, jackets, or sweatshirts on the backs of their chairs at the office (it's because temperature controls were designed for men wearing blazers). The key takeaway from the research is that one-size-fits-all leaves most of us out. We need to design our work for and from the margins, and in the process, we'll still get everyone else. Their principles are:

- ► Define equality
- ► Unearth inequities
- ► Learn from diversity
- ► Solve for one, benefit all

When we apply the Inclusive Design Principles through a communications approach, the principles can turn into:

- ► Define equity in DEI Communications
- ► Unearth inequities, majority coding, and exclusivity
- ► Learn from diversity across the team and in relationships
- ► Solve for one, benefit all

The benefit of structuring DEI communications this way is that it becomes a habit by embedding it into our processes. We are replacing a habit of unconscious bias with a habit of conscious unbias. We want

---

[77] "Korn Ferry | Organizational Consulting." www.kornferry.com.

to build the skills and processes to be as inclusive as possible so that we can help our people see and experience the value of that process.

The ultimate goal is to design DEI communications strategy for the most marginalized of our populations. When we design for the 20%, we will also get the 80%. This is known as the Curb Cut Effect, as defined in the Stanford Social Innovation Review, "Laws and programs designed to benefit vulnerable groups, such as the disabled or people of color, often end up benefiting all of society."[78] Think about how reducing the height of curbs has benefitted many beyond the targeted audience: wheelchair users, a group typically left out of infrastructure design. Other people with disabilities also benefit, from cane users and those who have had strokes, to cyclists and people pulling luggage or pushing carts or strollers. Everyone benefits when the most historically neglected are centered in design and decision making.

Consider what this looks like in the communications process: editorial planning, channels selection, adding accessibility features, ensuring visual inclusion, and being intentional about who is missing from the room when content is created, reviewed, or approved.

IDENTIFY CHECKPOINTS TO EMBED DEI INTO PROCESSES

After a year of intensive work, a company launched its updated website. The careers page featured three images: a young Black man in a customer service role; a mid-40s, white female in a corporate role; and an Indian man and Asian woman wearing glasses and sitting together to represent tech and engineering roles. In the proactive stage, the company was aware enough to seek visibly diverse representation, checking all the boxes with different skin tones, genders, and ages. Eventually, someone

---

[78] "The Curb-Cut Effect (SSIR)." Ssir.org. Accessed April 26, 2020. https://ssir.org/articles/entry/the_curb_cut_effect.

added employee belonging stories and information about joining ERGs.

At a minimum, this project involved copywriters, photographers, employee models, designers, reviewers, approvers, and publishers. Yet, despite all the time, energy, and money expended to update the site, ultimately candidates saw stereotypes. DEI communications probably wasn't at the beginning of their process, and there were no checkpoints along the way to challenge the majority coding.

A simple fix: re-associate the pictures with different jobs. For example, why not depict the young Black man in the corporate or engineering role? When the oversights were brought to the team's attention, they chose to keep the site as it was.

Without checkpoints, unconscious bias can slip in. Checkpoints make us accountable for our messaging. We can embed them in all parts of the process, from design to the content calendar. For example, if there is an article on protecting the environment, what about including something about protecting Indigenous lands? It's not always about adding more, but simply seeing and doing what we do through a DEI LENS.

When we start working on that deliverable due Friday, we can look at it from a different angle. Even if DEI is part of the process from the start, we can pause to ask questions at certain milestones. To help with accountability, we can embed diversity checkpoints in the communications process and set conditions for continuing by using a checklist like the following:

✓ Have we applied all aspects of The DEPTH Model?

✓ Can the story and visuals be more representative?

✓ Is the language inclusive?

✓ Does it tell an untold story from an authentic perspective?

✓ Are there stereotypes or nuances we need to replace?

✓ Does it acknowledge, accommodate, or empathize with different perspectives and/or experiences?

✓ Is there anything in the content that creates othering, us vs. them, separation, or a power dynamic?

The AP Stylebook has added inclusive storytelling with this context and purpose:

> Inclusive storytelling seeks to truly represent all people around the globe. It gives voice and visibility to those who have been missing or misrepresented in traditional narratives of both history and daily journalism. It helps readers and viewers both to recognize themselves in our stories, and to better understand people who differ from them in race, age, gender, class, and many other ways. It makes our work immeasurably stronger, more relevant, more compelling, more trustworthy.
>
> Inclusive storytelling should be part of everyday conversations, decision-making, and coverage. That means integrating these goals in all aspects of conversations, from the beginning of the story idea to garnering reaction (and more story ideas) after publication. Being an inclusive storyteller calls on all of us to stretch beyond our accustomed ways of thinking, our usual sources, our regular, go-to topics or angles for coverage. It challenges us to recognize and examine our unconscious biases and find ways to overcome them. It aims to infuse every aspect of coverage, both in text and in visuals, with diverse voices and faces, perspectives and context. It is considerate of language, sources, and diverse audiences. It often relies on teamwork and collaboration.[79]

The more we embed DEI and social justice content into our daily lives, the faster and easier it becomes to practice, and the more

---

[79] "Associated Press Stylebook." n.d. www.apstylebook.com.

impactful our content will be. Make no mistake, there's urgency around all of this.

STRUCTURING THE TEAM

What kind of team do we need? First, have a DEI communications expert with the ability to build a team, with the actual role and title; not a side hustle. That team then builds relationships with people throughout the organization who are skilled or are willing to learn DEI LENS skills. They can be a valuable resource.

And finally, the product of the first two parts of the team is the understanding that it is everyone in communication's responsibility to practice DEI. Every team member has DEI communications as part of their business goals.

In a perfect world, the head of DEI has a DEI communications team with budgets and goals. The DEI communications team is embedded across the organization in all of the organization's divisions.

DEI Communications Organization Chart

Chief Executive Officer

Chief Diversity Officer

DEI Communications Team
(Director, Sr. Manager, Manager, Specialists/Coordinators, and Interns)

- Embedded role in each department and region to focus on department objectives and regional DEI nuances
- Works with ERG communications contacts, diversity council/committee/task force
- Works with internal communications, HR communications, external communications, ESG/CSR communications
- Works with people manager communications
- Works with marketing, brand, copywriting, sales, and training on inclusive communications

No head of DEI?

Corporate Communications
All team members trained and accountable for a DEI lens on their work

The Conscious Communicator
The fine art of not saying stupid sh*t

For a downloadable copy of this graphic, please visit https://theconsciouscommunicator.com/

But, as we all know, our world is far from perfect. If there isn't a head of DEI, then start by investing in communicators learning how to do their everyday work with DEI lenses, mindsets and skill sets. Then, make a plan to build a DEI communications-specific role. If we are not consciously communicating, we likely are unconsciously causing harm. When we delay in learning and applying DEI communication skills to our work, we risk damaging our credibility as part of the voice of the organization.

To have DEPTH in our DEI communications practice, we must hire people committed to applying a DEI LENS. The result is a balanced team of people who can bring a variety of professional and life experience and skills to the work. When hiring for communicators, make sure to role model inclusive language in the job description and add a bullet point seeking someone with a growth mindset. Be very transparent that DEI is core to the communication's teams work. Building a balanced team takes intentionality. If there isn't an immediate role to hire, look at internship opportunities, partner with mid-level career return organizations, or bring in interim contractors and fight for the headcount.

Homogeneity limits a team's creative possibilities, and increases the potential for communicating stupid sh*t. As the stakes get higher, the consequences of imbalanced teams will only increase. The example of the stereotyped pictures on the career website begs three questions: 1) Did no one see this? 2) Did someone see this but stay silent? 3) Did somebody, or even multiple people, see something and say something, only to be overruled, or did their feedback never make it to decision-makers? Perhaps the team wasn't diverse enough to have the necessary psychological safety to voice concerns. Whatever the reason, the negative result is there for the world to see and for candidates to experience. We must heed what we hear from people who know what they're talking about, believe them, and take action on what they say.

Here's another story: a DEI consultant, who identifies as Asian American, was working on messaging for her clients around stopping anti-Asian hate. One of the organizations she was working with wanted to use the term Asian American Pacific Islander (AAPI) because other companies were. It's true that many community organizations use that term. It is, however, driven by the U.S. census, and it's a very broad grouping of a whole lot of countries, cultures, languages, customs, and identities. Because of that, it may not be an accurate shorthand for all who identify as Asian, Asian American, or Pacific Islander. Plus, it's well documented that people from Asia and Pacific Islanders have unique experiences based in oppression.[80]

This consultant was guiding communications when she brought this point up, and recommended tailoring the messaging to Asian and Asian American people. Remember, she identifies as Asian American, so she was speaking from her own personal and lived experience as well as that of being a DEI communicator who knows about inclusive language and tailoring messaging. In the end, the leaders ignored her recommendation and went with AAPI.

When we don't listen to the people who have these personal and professional experiences, we miss out on opportunities to learn. We don't know more than the people who are part of the communities we're creating messaging for. We need to trust the people who are living the experiences about which we are messaging. And we need to understand that perhaps these lumped groups, meant to put a whole bunch of different kinds of people under one umbrella, don't work. Seldom are the umbrella terms for populations chosen by the populations they describe. They were created as part of majority coding, so we need to gather input and ask impacted and involved groups to tell

---

[80] "Combating Anti-Asian Hate." n.d. Accessed June 21, 2022. https://www.aapihatecrimes.org.

their story. To quote the disability movement's powerful call to action, nothing about us without us.[81]

One aspect of diversity people reference when talking about teams: diversity of thought. While it's true diversity of thought produces better ideas and forces team members to think more when challenged, diversity of thought isn't a protected class. We can have homogeneity and still have diversity of thought.

The goal is not to bring in a variety of people for them to assimilate. It's to get us closer to that diverse, equitable, and inclusive workplace that doesn't yet exist.

There also are a variety of checkpoints useful for managing people:

✓ Who is on the team?

✓ Where are we seeking interns year-round?

✓ How and to whom do they report?

✓ Who's doing the writing?

✓ How diversified is our leadership?

✓ Is everyone checking for misalignment with our vision?

✓ What voices are represented?

✓ What images are used? Do we need different stock image libraries?

✓ Are stereotypes busted or reinforced?

✓ Are we tokenizing our current employees?

✓ Are we using inclusive language?

Above all else, train the team, partners, and stakeholders already in place. Build DEI into team goals, put DEI in the beginning of all

---

[81] Charlton, James I. *Nothing About Us Without Us: Disability Oppression and Empowerment.* University of California Press, 2000.

strategic planning, make DEI a part of performance conversations and measurement, give people room to learn, to make mistakes, and to improve. Build those internal relationships with DEI councils, ERGs, corporate social responsibility (CSR) partner organizations, and keep learning, changing, and going. Stay the course, and be proud of building a new legacy. One day we'll be able to say, yeah, I was there and I did that.

KEY TAKEAWAYS

1. Pushback is natural and we can stay resilient and committed to progress.

2. If we want the benefits of DEI communications in our work, we must embed DEI into our processes from the beginning.

3. We need teams that can co-create inclusive design principles into our communication practices.

Diversity, Equity, and Inclusion are Outcomes

by Lily Zheng

The Diversity, Equity, and Inclusion space has a metaphor problem, where flowery language in feel-good slogans obscures organizations' and practitioners' aversion to operationalizing "the work." These one-liners feel good to read and sound good when said, but follow up by asking, "Now what?" and they fall apart. When sayings like these are used as the foundation of the work, the resulting follow-up is often flimsy and unfocused.

I'll share with you the "sayings" I use in my work.

Diversity is an outcome. Either a space has achieved diversity on the basis of social dimensions (race, gender, class, sexuality, religion, ability, age, etc.) on every level, or it hasn't. The level of diversity that is "enough" is decided by stakeholders, and often centers on representational parity in a population. For every dimension on which an organization lacks diversity, organizational leaders must work to understand the nuances of why, and problem-solve until diversity is achieved.

Inclusion is an outcome. Either a space is one where people from valued identities and backgrounds all feel respect and empowered, or it isn't. The identities and backgrounds that are "valued" are decided by stakeholders, and often exclude identities that promote the exclusion of others (e.g. Neo-Nazis). For every dimension on which an organization lacks inclusion, organizational leaders must work to understand the nuances of why, and problem-solve until inclusion is achieved.

Equity is an outcome. Either a space ensures that all people have the tools and resources they need to succeed, have their employment needs met, are rewarded fairly for their work, and do not experience abuse, discrimination, or mistreatment, or it doesn't. For every dimension on which an organization lacks equity, organizational leaders must work to understand the nuances of why, and problem-solve until equity is achieved.

Diversity is an outcome. Inclusion is an outcome. Equity is an outcome. If your organization hasn't achieved them, then it needs to keep going until it has.

These definitions are simple on purpose, so we can move on from them to do the far less simple work of achieving the outcomes they spell out. Any DEI initiative that wants to avoid the trap of stalling at the starting line would do well to use similar ones.

Biography

Lily Zheng (they/them) is a diversity, equity, and inclusion consultant who works with organizations to turn positive intentions into positive impact. They have written for the Harvard Business Review, Quartz at Work *and* HR Executive. *Lily is also the co-author of* Gender Ambiguity in the Workplace: Transgender and Gender-Diverse Discrimination, The Ethical Sellout: Maintaining Your Integrity in the Age of Compromise *and* DEI Deconstructed: Your No-Nonsense Guide to Doing the Work and Doing It Right.

CHAPTER 13

STRATEGY AND MEASUREMENT

You become responsible, forever, for what you have tamed.

—Antoine de Saint-Exupéry, The Little Prince

D EI communications is a skill set that every communicator should acquire. Organizations should hire people who specialize in this work, and like HR, IT, and Legal, embed DEI communications throughout the company.

DEI communicators craft the DEI communications strategy that advises the corporate communications strategy. Ideally, DEI communicators are part of a DEI communications team, led by a chief diversity officer who reports directly to the CEO.

In many ways, the DEI communications strategy sets content direction, determining its purpose. It tells us whose stories to center. It serves as the foundation for ongoing content. The maturity of a DEI communications strategy depends on the maturity of the company's

DEI strategy–the degree to which DEI goals are aligned with business goals, and company values, mission, and vision.

If DEI is integrated into the business, then it's easier to align DEI communications with the corporate communications strategy. From there, we can build content for social justice topics, heritage months, and more. However, we also should integrate DEI into all content, implicitly where it makes sense, and explicitly in the content's creation, approach, and consistent accessibility.

Part of building a DEI communications plan is defining its structure and determining its position within the workspace. This can be done separately, although not in isolation, as many communications can be. It then needs to be integrated into the full plan, touching every part of the business.

ELEMENTS OF A
DEI COMMUNICATIONS STRATEGY

Here's where it all comes together: articulating the vision with intention, tying to the organization's strategies, goals, and values, naming where communications is stepping up and being accountable as part of DEI work across the organization. The elements of a DEI communications strategy are:

- ► Introduction: DEI statement, narrative, story tied to company strategy and company DEI strategy, dimensions of diversity, definitions of diversity, equity, and inclusion

- ► DEI goals, objectives, priorities

- ► Definition of DEI communications, the role of communications in DEI, how communications supports overall DEI strategies and goals

- ► How to communicate: accessibility, approachability with plain language, human-centered, etc. (make sure this shows up the same way in the Brand guidelines)

- ▸ Key messages, target audiences, tactics, channels
- ▸ DEI-specific content calendar and editorial process co-created with DEI council and ERGs, roadmap
- ▸ Inclusive Communications Guide link, DEI trainings, DEI LENS (on what communications controls)
- ▸ Ongoing learning, listening, feedback loops, infrastructure, budget, process, policies, team

Be sure to focus on those who manage people. Managers typically are not promoted because they have amazing communication skills (just like leaders). As part of strategy, have a specific effort to train, support, and resource people managers. Here's an example from Adobe:

> Essential education from microaggressions to unconscious bias to psychological safety.

> Adobe For All In Action people manager guidelines: Leading For All Toolkit for creating inclusive practices within teams, guidance for building team inclusion given the COVID-19 pandemic and racial injustices, and advice for handling team discussions in a sensitive manner.[82]

INCLUSIVE COMMUNICATIONS GUIDES AND DEI STATEMENTS

Inclusive language, as defined by the Linguistic Society of America, "acknowledges diversity, conveys respect to all people, is sensitive to differences, and promotes equal opportunities."[83] Add flexibility, non-judgment, accuracy, and global relevance when an organization is global. And remember the earlier reference to softening language? Inclusive language expert Suzanne Wertheim, Ph.D. says, "My first

---

[82] "Diversity and Inclusion." www.adobe.com. n.d. https://www.adobe.com/diversity.html.

[83] "Guidelines for Inclusive Language | Linguistic Society of America." www.linguisticsociety.org. n.d. https://www.linguisticsociety.org/resource/guidelines-inclusive-language.

principle of inclusive language is that it accurately reflects reality. One sub-principle is "avoid using 'softening language,' which inappropriately softens problematic behavior and presents it as acceptable."" Inclusive language isn't always nice. It isn't about making everyone feel better. Instead, inclusive language is about pointing out truths, even if they make some people uncomfortable."[84]

Inclusive language can be criticized as being "woke," a term co-opted from the Black community and used as a pejorative in an attempt to stop people from learning, improving, and changing. As communicators, it's better to be awake than asleep, to lift up rather than harm others. We want people to know their names and identities are safe in our mouths and our work. This should be our legacy as conscious communicators.

Inclusive Communication Guides have two purposes:

- ▸ Internal: A reference guide for all employees to learn as needed, and to improve interpersonal, manager, team, and overall internal communications. Think of it as a social agreement to use respectful language.

- ▸ External: A reference guide for all content creators, ensuring they create inclusive and representative content, a companion to brand guidelines and employee handbooks.

At a minimum, the guide should include definitions, guidelines, explanations, and examples of microaggressions, phrases to avoid, and allyship resources. The guide is not meant to be exhaustive or include every term. It effectively addresses the most harmful and exclusive terms and language in communication. The guide helps make organizations more psychologically safe, mitigating unintentional harm by serving as a social agreement (there's that term again) of how people will treat each

[84] Wertheim, Suzanne Ph.D. Accessed May 27, 2022. https://www.linkedin.com/posts/suzanne-wertheim-ph-d-1508464_inclusivelanguage-ukraine-activity-6903119740781387776-La-7/?inf_contact_key=5987b9980a8560f853f1ec3a9f49e522&utm_medium=member_desktop_web&utm_source=linkedin_share.

other through language. Here's the kicker: language shapes behavior, so an inclusive language guide can establish DEI expectations in a way that encourages and enables participation by all.

A companion to brand and writing style guidelines, employee handbooks or codes of conduct, the inclusive communications guide informs social media directives, crisis communications plans, social justice guidelines, diversity reports, CSR, environment, social, and governance (ESG), and event/conference speaker vetting processes. The guide touches every part of the organization, including and beyond communications: marketing, human resources, sales scripts, product documentation, customer care greetings, technical terms in programming… everything.

Words can hurt or heal. Divide or unite. Doing or saying nothing maintains the status quo. Doing nothing is still a decision. It is still taking a position. It's still heard, felt, and remembered. One of the differences between corporate communications team members and employees is what they pay attention to. For example, when external forces or internal implosions happen, leaders and communicators go into fire drill mode. We scramble, we react, we post that post and send that email. Then we wipe our foreheads, dust off our hands, and move on to the next thing.

Employees, however, do not. They see the patterns. That email we just sent wasn't a one-off, but one of many examples they filed away—one piece of a larger conversation.

Employees pay much closer attention to what we say than we might think. An operative DEI statement can help us say the right things.

Think about it, doesn't it seem that 90% of any DEI initiative, department, or work is communications? We are a huge part of this work, whether communicating internally among the different factions building programs or sharing externally the things we're doing. It's our job to make the DEI vision a reality. How much more effective might we be if we also helped shape that vision?

Every organization needs a DEI statement. Current and prospective employees, customers, communities, and suppliers—they all expect the statement to be on the company's website and operating within the organization. This calls for an *operative* DEI statement, and The DEPTH Model can help communicators create it.

Operative DEI statements are actionable statements appropriately operationalized across the organization. The operative word is actionable.

Imagine this: On the quarterly earnings call, the CEO says, "Merger and acquisition is part of our growth strategy. It's a journey, but we'll get there." The call is over, the statement is going viral, the stock and the CEO's job is tanking. That's stupid sh*t a CEO would never say.

However, if this same CEO said, "DEI is a journey, but we'll get there," few people would blink. Never mind that the message shows a lack of urgency and accountability; no understanding of DEI as a business driver; and zero respect for underrepresented people's lived experiences and history—including the employees who work to benefit these same leaders.

Anatomy of a DEI Statement

The DEI statement is a vision and mission that communicates the organization's priorities and shapes its action. It should be a unique, stand-alone statement, but it should support and help advance the organization's overall vision and mission.

The DEI statement asks three questions:

1. Why are we doing this?
2. What are we going to do?
3. How are we going to do it?

The answers plug into the following format:

- Because we believe…
- We will…
- By…

The first statement is the vision, the why. The second and third statements—the what and how—are the mission. The mission may change as the organization delivers on the what and how. The vision is evergreen; it's the organization's aspiration.

Draft the statement, then check it against The DEPTH Model, asking if it is:

- Deliberate, with a clear "why"
- Educated, because we've done our research to make sure our "what" is right and realistic.
- Purposeful, as in aligned with our company mission and vision.
- Tailored, with a "how" that we are best equipped to do.
- Habitual, something we can and will commit to doing consistently.

Choose and embody language that will lead to the desired outcomes. Use the same language around DEI as you would around all strategic business goals—seriousness, commitment, value, urgency, and accountability. Because DEI communication is all of those things.

MEASUREMENT

Every effective business strategy has metrics that are meaningful to the organization. The measurement and monitoring needed for effective DEI communications starts with the questions: "What is it that we're trying to do?" "Why are we stepping into this space?" "What do we hope to achieve?" Once we know that, we can look at tools that are already in place and repurpose those that could be tweaked. In departments like product or marketing, very mature measurement tools are in place. Even for social and PR, there are very meticulous analytics. This does not mean that they are automatically good at measuring the achievement of your vision.

As communicators, we need to look at:

1. What we control (content, visuals)
2. How we distribute (accessibility, channel mix, tools)
3. Impact (behavior change, actions taken by audience)

The standard numbers that we see from the big consulting firms state that businesses with more diverse organizations are 35% more effective and have higher profit margins, but this is correlation without causation. We don't *know* that these standards are true, because we don't measure them. To really make the true business case for diversity, a couple of things have to happen. First of all, people have to truly believe diversity has value. If they truly believe it does, then they'll treat it like an asset, nurturing it and putting resources behind it. A vicious cycle happens when people don't do this: they can never prove that diversity is truly a valuable resource. The companies that believe in the value are the ones that will start the process of saying, "We believe in it, and we'll measure it." And when measured, that's going to mean creating new measurement systems to help us understand impact, opportunities, and insights.

For example, if we want to figure out what diversity does, the first question to ask is, "What are we solving by focusing on diversity?" If we haven't asked that question, then we have no way of knowing where we're going to start measuring. But if we ask that question and, for example, answer it with, "We're solving for innovation," then we can figure out how innovation happens in the organization.

Once we know that, we can determine the touch points where innovation gets from somebody's brain into actual practice and start measuring the role of diversity, what its contribution is, and what its absence or presence is in all those places. Then we can actually connect diversity to outcomes. When we do that, we prove that diversity has value.

Once we've examined our current measurement tools, we can build and invest in new tools that will help us measure anything we choose, from A to Z. It sounds ridiculous, but one metric for communicators used to be inches of copy. However, a lot of our current metrics are equally useless because they don't change people's experiences in the workplace. For example, if we focus solely on hiring and don't pay attention to pay equity, promotion pacing, retention, and exit interviews, then we turnstile people right out of the company. We may celebrate all these people we're bringing in, but they don't stay. We're not telling the truth because there's a lifecycle story there that we're ignoring.

Communicators seldom have the budget and resources to collect a lot of data. HR does, however. So do marketing, product development, and customer service. Advocate for funding, or partner with other teams, but don't continue to invest in irrelevant metrics that don't get us any closer to our vision.

Measurement should inspire movement. Advocate for public sharing of metrics and tell their story. Remember that is one of our skills as communicators: visibility drives accountability. What are we tolerating that is counterproductive to the DEI communications strategy, our business goals, organizational values, and purpose of the company?

This brings us to the intersection of vision and metrics. If we don't have a vision yet, start somewhere and say, "This is what we did, and we don't like the result. Why was this bad? How did this happen?" Channel the inner two-year-old self and keep asking "why" questions until we get to something that we can do to correct the problems we've uncovered. Otherwise, our efforts become bandages for avoidance and we'll repeat the same issues a day, week, month, or even a year later. That's time we can't get back, talent that we've lost, and a reputation that we can't fix.

We may not be able to eliminate people's unconscious biases, but we can build systems to make them accountable for their behavior in our space. Focusing on what we can change and influence, we build systems of accountability and measurement. Each organization already does this, so it's not new. We monitor the company credit cards, we cannot spend our department's budget at the bar, IT knows when we log on and how long we've been logged on. The measurement and monitoring needed for effective DEI communications should be no different. Start by cleaning up corporate language and measure the moments that matter:

- ▸ Moments of decision
- ▸ Moments of inclusion
- ▸ Moments of visibility
- ▸ Moments of representation
- ▸ Moments of engagement
- ▸ Moments of belonging
- ▸ Moments of giving/donating

This technique leads to DEI becoming infused in values and organizational goals.

KEY TAKEAWAYS

1. Establish DEI communications strategy as its own thing, but tie it to the corporate communications strategy, company strategies, goals, and values.

2. Embed DEI communications plans and efforts across the business.

3. Measure the moments that matter to create movement that matter.

Targeted Universalism
The Othering and Belonging Institute

One method of measurement comes from the Othering and Belonging Institute at the University of California, Berkeley. Led by law professor john a. powell, they have designed a measurement system called *targeted universalism*:

> Targeted universalism means setting universal goals pursued by targeted processes to achieve those goals. Within a targeted universalism framework, universal goals are established for all groups concerned. The strategies developed to achieve those goals are targeted, based upon how different groups are situated within structures, culture, and across geographies to obtain the universal goal. Targeted universalism is goal oriented, and the processes are directed in service of the explicit, universal goal.[85]

Targeted Universalism is a platform to put into practice social programs that move all groups toward a universal policy goal. It supports the needs of the most marginalized groups, as well as those who are more politically powerful, while reminding everyone that we are all part of the same social fabric. Targeted universalism involves taking five steps:

- Set a universal goal
- Measure the overall population relative to the universal goal
- Measure population segments
- Understand structural and group-based factors
- Implement targeted strategies

If you have a goal to be fully representative in your photography, videography, and graphics, then you need to look at your systems, processes, and structures to understand why you haven't been representative already. This could mean

---

[85] "Targeted Universalism | Othering & Belonging Institute." Belonging.berkeley.edu. n.d. https://belonging.berkeley.edu/targeted-universalism.

limiting your stock image libraries that are not fully inclusive and representative. Maybe they don't include people with physical disabilities, people above the age of 50, transgender people, or a variety of body types and sizes. Then you target your solutions. You either seek a more diverse set of stock image libraries to balance out the options or do your own in-house recordings in partnership with ERGs or the diversity council. By targeting specific solutions for removing barriers that exclude or underrepresent people from your visuals, you are making progress in reaching the universal goal of full representation.

CHAPTER 14

FOCUS ON THE OUTCOME

We must always take sides.
Neutrality helps the oppressor, never the victim.
Silence encourages the tormentor, never the tormented.

—Elie Wiesel, writer, professor, political activist,
Nobel laureate, and Holocaust survivor

Here's the truth: Yes, applying DEI to communications work is relatively new as a discipline, it's not how we've been trained and it's not how we've historically been rewarded. However, we see the future and the future looks like embedding DEI into communications practices and companies taking firm stands on social justice. And for good reason: employees no longer are willing to accept organizational silence on exclusion and social justice issues. Indeed, in a Harvard Business Review article titled, "Employees Are Sick of Being Asked to Make Moral Compromises," the authors note the importance of this shift:

The pandemic and resulting upheaval of the workplace have shone a bright spotlight on organizational experiences we've too long written off as mere annoyances or ineffective management. But as it turns out, their consequences can be more damaging than we understood. The mass exodus from our workplaces is, in part, a proclamation that people can't—and won't—tolerate mistreatment, injustice, and incompetence from their leaders anymore, particularly at the expense of their dignity and values. Organizational conditions that give rise to moral injury violate our sense of justice, which according to some social science theories is hardwired into our brains. This means that perceptions of justice (or injustice) in the workplace have profound effects on employees.[86]

If this is the new normal, communicators have an incredible opportunity to use our talents and gifts to sustain DEI communications and social justice work.

Think about it. We can send an email to 100,000 people around the globe with one press of the "send" button. We can create graphics for social posts that reach millions of people with a press of the "publish" button. Think of what we might accomplish if we did what we do with a DEI LENS . We have power and influence over how employees feel about the company they work for and how customers feel about buying our products and services. They need to know that we will give them a voice, that we will be intentionally inclusive with our words, speak for basic human rights, and make a positive impact in society. And above all, they must know that we will honor their human dignity, recognize their strengths, and celebrate their unique identities. When we do that, people who aren't employees have the opportunity for the same protections. Our influence extends beyond the walls of the companies we work for.

---

[86] Carucci, Ron, and Praslova, Ludmila N. "Employees Are Sick of Being Asked to Make Moral Compromises." Harvard Business Review. Accessed February 21, 2022.

Here's how we use our superpowers:

- Lead introspective discussions to embed The DEPTH Model within our organizations

- Partner with marketing, brand, sales, training, HR, customer care, etc.

- Build a DEI communications strategy

- Review processes and embed DEI from the beginning

- Build a balanced team

- Build a DEI infrastructure of stakeholders, ERGs, councils, and external partners

- Build a communication plan

- Establish an advisory role with leadership

- Secure funding

PAYING FOR DEI—NOW OR LATER?

Protecting the company starts with protecting its employees by honoring them. Something we often hear is, "I can't afford a line item for DEI communications." While tough financial decisions are a reality of business, we have to invest in DEI communications like any other business communication transformation. A lot of companies claim to put employees first. One way to do that is by funding DEI communications to stay relevant, grow, and attract the talent we need to stay competitive and innovative.

We need to have the systems, processes, policies, practices, and personnel in place to back us. Companies pay for DEI on the backend, with big buckets of money for legal teams to cover discrimination and harassment lawsuits. The U.S. Equal Employment Opportunity Commission receives approximately $404 million dollars from U.S. employers every year to cover these lawsuits. They further estimate that it costs between $5,000 and $10,000 dollars to replace an hourly worker who has left after discriminatory practices.[87] That cost goes up to between $75,000 and $211,000 to replace an executive.[88]

Now, few legal or HR departments would willingly surrender some of their budget to fund DEI communications, but that mindset is part of the problem. Once we reach the point where we're replacing employees and we need the bucket of lawsuit money, it's too late. This is where we change the narrative to help those with budget authority to see that DEI communications is in fact a company-protecting investment as well. Why not reallocate these or other funds before someone leaves? Our companies don't have a supply problem. Our companies have a distribution problem.

Communicators can help organizations examine DEI policies and practices for what they say about the culture, giving company policy makers insight into ways to align those practices with what the company stands for. The result: better employee engagement, higher productivity, potentially fewer lawsuits from a workforce that feels safe, seen, heard, and valued.

FOCUS ON THE OUTCOME

It's true that DEI can become emotionally charged, which makes sense. Diversity, equity, and inclusion work is about identities, about people. Many organizations that claim to be employee-first or people-centered make business decisions that are anything but. That's not surprising, because most organizations reflect the dominant culture; they aren't designed to include all people, in all the ways people can show up. And the further one deviates from the established standard, the harder it can

---

[87] "EEOC Releases Fiscal Year 2020 Enforcement and Litigation Data | U.S. Equal Employment Opportunity Commission." www.eeoc.gov. Accessed February 26, 2021.

[88] "The Costly Business of Discrimination." The Center for American Progress. n.d. www.americanprogress.org/article/the-costly-business-of-discrimination.

be to function in a workplace built on that standard. DEI work helps close the gap and re-imagine the standard. DEI communications is a solution, outcome, and catalyst for organizations to meet and beat their business goals.

Differences between people are not the problem. It's the polarization around differences that cause the problems. We manufacture the problems, we construct them—which means we can deconstruct them. As conscious communicators, with awareness of others' experiences and a commitment to centering them, we are uniquely positioned to help build a truly people-centered workplace. That work starts with shared language and shared outcomes.

When we focus on shared outcomes, we lower people's defenses and help them see the benefits of diversity. Ask the team, "What are we solving for with DEI communications?" Clarify this as part of the work with the "why." Focus on the outcome of DEI work and its benefit for everyone, and even the dominant majority will gain in a more welcoming, respectful, and appreciative workplace.

THE IMPACT OF DEI COMMUNICATIONS

We've established the problem, but we also need to understand the risks of inaction, defending the status quo, pretending that DEI communications isn't our job, or isn't a priority. As communicators, we are complicit in the harm caused by performative communications, microaggressions, reinforcing stereotypes in our content, and contributing to damaging our brand's reputation.

Here's a partial list of real-world business consequences:

▸ Brand reputation damage, PR, and crisis communications

▸ Unwanted attrition (The Great Resignation)

▸ Productivity loss, disengagement, absenteeism

▸ Mental health impact

- Protests, employee walkouts, boycotts
- Lawsuits, HR resources/employee relations
- Customer churn
- Loss of market share
- Product/service fails, inaccessibility, exclusion
- Shareholder criticism and board pressure
- Stock market/investor/government contracts cost

Many organizations are on board with DEI communications, but hesitant to engage on social justice issues. However, DEI communications is the foundation of social justice communications with support from The DEPTH Model.

Diversity discussions are mandatory; social justice discussions are not. But inequity is at the heart of every social justice issue. The DEPTH Model helps us decide when and what we could and should say. The language of DEI is the language of equity, which is the language of social justice.

The demographics of the world are changing. Communication teams must be representative to inform inclusive communications, reflect audiences, and speak from a place of education and authority. We can influence policy. We can change the narrative. We can bring DEPTH to our communications. We can effect change and help our companies and organizations do the good they are capable of doing. We are cut out for this and we are rising to the occasion. Let's communicate like we give a damn. Let's heed the call to help our leaders, our companies, our teams, and ourselves stop saying stupid sh*t.

*AI is neural in design,
not neutral by default.*

CHAPTER 15:

THE ALGORITHMIC ECHO CHAMBER

"The machines we build reflect the priorities, preferences, and prejudices of those who have the power to shape technology."

**– Dr. Joy Buolamwini, founder,
Algorithmic Justice League**

As conscious communicators, we work to be aware of the impact our words can have. But what do we do when the very tools we use to communicate—from chatbots to content generators—are tainted by bias?

In Chapter 2, we explored the minefield of unconscious bias in human communication—those ingrained prejudices we carry within us that can unwittingly sabotage our messages and relationships. We learned how to recognize our own biases, challenge them, and strive for communication that is as fair and inclusive as possible.

Today, however, the communication landscape has evolved. Artificial intelligence, in its various forms, has become an increasingly ubiquitous tool in our arsenal. From grammar checkers and plagiarism detectors to content generators and social media management tools, AI offers undeniable advantages in efficiency and reach. Yet, as with any powerful tool, it comes with its own set of ethical challenges.

ARTIFICIAL INTELLIGENCE, REAL BIAS

AI learns from the world around us, so it inherits the biases that exist in our society, both contemporary and historical.

As early as the '70s and up through the 2000s, we saw the rise of predictive AI. [89] It started making big calls—who could get a loan, who might be a criminal. The problem was, it learned from historical data, and that data was often biased. Imagine an area that was heavily policed in the past, maybe unfairly so. The AI, looking at that data, might label it a high-crime zone even if things had changed. It's the beginning of digital redlining, perpetuating systemic biases.

Fast forward to the 2010s. Generative AI is making art, writing stories, and even helping companies decide who to hire or promote— all based, ultimately, on those older, biased models. [90]

Generative AI, like Large Language Models (LLMS), can be incredibly powerful. However, they also can perpetuate and amplify biases from their training data.[91] This can result in problematic outcomes, like marketing copy that reinforces harmful stereotypes or

---

89 O'Neil, C. (2016). Weapons of math destruction: How big data increases inequality and threatens democracy. Crown.

90 Bender, E. M., Gebru, T., McMillan-Major, A., & Shmitchell, S. (2021). On the Dangers of Stochastic Parrots: Can Language Models Be Too Big? Proceedings of the 2021 ACM Conference on Fairness, Accountability, and Transparency, 610–623.

91 Ibid..

customer service chatbots that misinterpret cultural nuances, leading to misunderstandings and potentially offensive interactions.[92] For instance, an AI trained primarily on Western data might inadvertently promote Eurocentric beauty standards or struggle to understand phrases common in African American Vernacular English (AAVE).

BIAS IS BAKED IN

Back in the days of early computing, there was a popular term, GIGO. It meant garbage in, garbage out. The term for the age of AI? BIBO: Bias in, bias out.

There are two kinds of "bad" inputs: Data that furthers misconceptions, and data that upholds dominant norms. Together, they create three types of bad data outputs: ingrained, insulting, and inaccurate.

Here are some examples we've seen personally:

Ingrained

Prompt: Example of a historical Black pioneer or inventor who faced challenges.

ChatGPT: "Thomas Edison invented the light bulb, but let's not forget the obstacles faced by inventors like him in a society marked by racial biases."

Ingrained bias perpetuates erasure of some folks' contributions to history and innovation. While the prompt specifically requests an example of a Black pioneer or inventor, ChatGPT defaulted to highlighting Thomas Edison, a white inventor. This suggests that the AI's training data and algorithms prioritize the accomplishments of

---

92 Blodgett, S. L., Green, L., & Schneider, B. (2020). Demographic dialectal variation in social media: A case study of African American English. Language Variation and Change, 32(2), 185–215.

white individuals, even when the context explicitly calls for recognition of Black achievements.

It's not just wrong. It's an example of systemic biases embedded within AI systems, reinforcing dominant narratives and overlooking the contributions of marginalized groups.

Insulting

Prompt 1: Write a LinkedIn post about the current DEI backlash from the perspective of a CDO.

ChatGPT: "DEI isn't about taking anything away from anyone. It's about making sure we all get a fair shot, no matter who we are or where we're from. Let's clear up any misunderstandings and remember what this is really about: fairness, opportunities, and a workplace that values everyone."

*Prompt 2: Make it from the perspective of a **Black** CDO.*

ChatGPT: "Change ain't easy. DEI isn't about taking from one to give to another. Nah, it's ensuring everybody gets a fair shot. Growth ain't always comfortable, right? In the words of our ancestors, 'If you want to go fast, go alone. If you want to go far, go together.'"

While the intention might be to create an authentic voice, doing so with stereotypical language and phrasing ("Change ain't easy," "Nah," "Growth ain't always comfortable," "In the words of our ancestors") is not the way–especially in a professional context like LinkedIn, where such generalizations can undermine the credibility and authority of the speaker.

Inaccurate

Prompt: What has Jennifer Richeson written about the browning of America?

Google Gemini: "Jennifer Richeson is a Yale psychologist and MacArthur genius. She has written about the browning of America. In her book, Brown is the New White ..."

Jennifer Richeson is a prominent scholar. She has researched and written about the implications of America's increasing racial and ethnic diversity. Her work explores themes related to the shifting demographics and their impact on social and political dynamics in the United States. She authored a Deeper Dive in this book. However, she didn't write Brown is the New White. That was Steve Phillips.

As Meredith Whittaker, co-founder and co-director of NYU's AI Now Institute starkly put it, AI "is, and ... inextricably will be, replicating patterns of historical inequality and marginalization. And in many powerful ways, it will be obscuring accountability for those decisions." [93]

If the AI can't be held accountable because it relies on biased training data, then where does the responsibility lie? It falls squarely on us, the conscious communicators.

IT'S ALL ON US

So, what can we do?

First, acknowledge the issue. AI bias is real, and it can seep into our work. Second, choose AI tools carefully. Research their ethics and transparency. Third, always scrutinize AI-generated content. Question its language, representation, and potential biases. Fourth, provide

93 Bursztynsky, J. (2023, June 15). Meredith Whittaker believes AI is 'replicating patterns of inequality. *Fast Company.* https://www.fastcompany.com/90908974/why-meredith-whittaker-believes-ai-is-replicating-patterns-of-inequality

feedback when you see bias. Help the AI learn and improve. Finally, remember that AI is a tool, not a replacement for human judgment. Use it wisely, and always keep your commitment to conscious communication at the forefront.

As communicators, we must be vigilant, questioning the outputs of AI tools just as critically as we scrutinize our own words. Here are some red flags to watch out for:

► Language that reinforces stereotypes: Does the AI consistently use gendered language when describing certain professions? Does it rely on harmful tropes when depicting different racial or ethnic groups?

► Lack of representation: Does the AI struggle to generate diverse images or examples? Does it default to a narrow range of perspectives?

► Unequal treatment: Does the AI exhibit different behaviors or provide different results based on factors like gender, race, or origin?

Remember, AI bias isn't always overt. It often reveals itself in subtle ways, requiring us to pay close attention and ask critical questions.

AI is both an exciting opportunity and a complex challenge. We can dream of AI systems that recognize and correct their own biases, but, for now, the responsibility rests with us, the humans behind the algorithms.

As communicators, we have a crucial role to play in shaping the future of AI. By approaching these tools with a critical eye and a commitment to inclusion, we can harness the power of AI while mitigating its potential harms. We can ensure that our messages, whether crafted by human hands or algorithmic assistance, contribute to a more just and equitable world. We can make sure AI isn't saying stupid sh*t.

KEY TAKEAWAYS

1. AI isn't neutral; it's as biased as we are.

2. We are responsible for the ethical use of AI and its impact on communications.

3. Combat AI bias by being critical, demanding transparency, and prioritizing conscious communication.

.

Every crisis is a test of values.

CHAPTER 16:

COMMUNICATING IN THE EYE OF THE STORM

"What fresh hell is this?"

– Dorothy Parker, writer, journalist, poet, satirist, and Broadway playwright

We've always had crises. But before the internet, social media, and an always-on, gluttonous news cycle, there seemed at least to be some sort of break between them. When emotions run high and the pressure to respond is immediate, thoughtful consideration is a luxury communicators can't afford. In crisis, The DEPTH Model may be the difference between taking a stand or falling flat.

WHY WE SAY STUPID SH*T IN THE FIRST PLACE

Humans naturally view the world through moral lenses, often resorting to black-and-white thinking, especially when confronted with emotionally charged situations.[94] This is further complicated by:

- ▶ Moral outrage, which leads us instinctively to judge, fueled by a desire for justice, or in some cases, vengeance.[95]

- ▶ Bias, often unconscious, that colors our perceptions and influences our reactions.[96]

- ▶ Oversimplification, because our brains crave simplicity. Grappling with complex issues like systemic racism or religious conflict is hard, so we tend to oversimplify narratives and ignore systemic factors.[97]

In crisis, leaders and organizations really just feel the need to engage, either to live up to their values or respond to their stakeholders. Innate responses are totally natural, but they can lead to knee-jerk reactions and ultimately, saying stupid sh*t. And while it's one thing to do that as an individual, it's a much bigger problem when an organization or a leader does it—especially in a crisis.

---

94 Cikara, M., Bruneau, E. G., & Saxe, R. (2020). Their pain gives us pleasure: How intergroup dynamics shape empathic failures and counter-empathic responses. Journal of Personality and Social Psychology, 118(6), 1135–1163.

95 Brady, W. J., Crockett, M. J., & Van Bavel, J. J. (2022). The MAD model of moral contagion: How moral emotions spread through networks. Trends in Cognitive Sciences, 26(1), 68–78.

96 Meissner, C. A., Wang, C., & Wheatley, T. (2023). The neuroscience of implicit bias. Annual Review of Psychology, 74, 401–427.

97 Fiske, S. T., Cikara, M., & Cuddy, A. J. (2017). Why ordinary people torture enemy prisoners. Proceedings of the National Academy of Sciences, 113(20), 5492–5497.

CLARITY AMID CHAOS

This is where The DEPTH model becomes invaluable, providing a framework for conscious communication that acknowledges our human tendencies and helps us navigate crises with greater intentionality:

- ▶ **Deliberate:** "Do we have a clear, articulable goal for stepping out on this?" This question forces us to move beyond emotional reactions to define a solid communication objective. Are we expressing solidarity, offering support, or simply acknowledging the situation? Clarity helps mitigate the risk of the message being misconstrued or hijacked by emotional biases.

- ▶ **Educated:** "Do we know all we need to know about this?" This is where we combat our brain's tendency to oversimplify. Are we taking the time to understand the historical context, the nuances of the situation, and the various perspectives involved before commenting on complex issues? Remember, acknowledging complexity isn't about condoning violence; it's about engaging with the issue responsibly.

- ▶ **Purposeful:** "Does this align with our mission and vision?" This question ensures an authentic response instead of a reaction to external pressure. Consider a company whose mission statement emphasizes diversity and inclusion. Staying silent on an issue like the 2022 Buffalo shooting, rooted in racial hatred, would contradict their stated values and ring hollow to their audience. [98]

- ▶ **Tailored:** "How can we craft a message that resonates with our specific audience while minimizing harm?" This goes beyond simply considering the impact on stakeholders; it's

---

98   Wikipedia.   (n.d.).   2022   Buffalo   shooting.   https://en.wikipedia.org/wiki/2022_Buffalo_shooting

about actively shaping the message to suit the context. Which communication channels are appropriate? What language is sensitive and inclusive? What information is necessary to provide? This requires understanding cultural nuances and potential sensitivities, as well as your organization's relevance to the issue. Always consider how you can advance the message in a unique but not self-serving way.

- ▸ **Habitual:** "Is this part of our ongoing commitment to DEI or social justice, or a reactive, one-off response?" This is crucial for assessing authenticity and impact. Has the organization engaged—consistently—with the issue or issues like it? For all groups? What will it do the next time? The time after that? If this time is different, can we explain why?

MASTERING THE UNPREDICTABLE

Crises, by their very nature, defy prediction. They erupt without warning, demanding swift action in a landscape charged with emotion and uncertainty. In these moments, our instinctive responses, shaped by moral lenses, outrage, bias, and the urge to simplify, can lead us astray.

But amidst the chaos, there's opportunity. The DEPTH model serves as a compass, guiding us towards communication that's deliberate, informed, authentic, and impactful. By consciously applying its principles, we can transcend knee-jerk reactions and emerge from crises with integrity and purpose.

In a world where the news cycle never sleeps and the stakes are high, mastering the unpredictable is not just an aspiration—it's a necessity.

APPLYING DEPTH TO REAL-WORLD SCENARIOS

Let's see how three different fictional companies might handle the Israel-Hamas conflict using the DEPTH model.

Company A: Tech Startup

- ▸ **Profile:** Young, scrappy, and wants to change the world. They talk a big DEI/social justice game, but they're still figuring it out internally.

- ▸ **DEPTH Analysis**

  - ▹ **Deliberate:** Support employees, reaffirm inclusivity, and avoid looking like hypocrites. **Score: 4**

  - ▹ **Educated:** Not directly tied to the conflict, but knows their employees come from all walks of life and bias is a no-no. **Score: 3**

  - ▹ **Purposeful:** DEI is a core value, so they see this as a chance to prove it's not just lip service. **Score: 4**

  - ▹ **Tailored:** Talk about the role of technology in war. Use their tech skills to share reliable info and maybe host some carefully moderated online discussions. **Score: 3**

  - ▹ **Habitual:** Still building their DEI track record, so people will be watching closely. **Score: 2**

- ▸ **Average DEPTH Score: 3.2**

- ▸ **Action:** Company A needs to walk the walk. Focus on their people first, make sure everyone feels safe. Share good info, create safe spaces for talking. They're still learning, so owning that is better than faking it.

Company B: Global Consumer Goods Company

- **Profile:** Big, established, and all about protecting that brand. They say they care about DEI, but they don't like rocking the boat.

- **DEPTH Analysis:**

  - ▷ **Deliberate:** Don't piss anyone off, keep the brand safe, maybe say as little as possible. **Score: 2**

  - ▷ **Educated:** They know this is a minefield, so they're trying to understand things before they act. **Score: 4**

  - ▷ **Purposeful:** DEI vs. staying neutral … tough call. They might end up looking like hypocrites. **Score: 2**

  - ▷ **Tailored:** Not much room to maneuver, probably some generic "we support peace" stuff. **Score: 2**

  - ▷ **Habitual:** If their past actions don't match their DEI talk, they're in trouble. **Score: 1**

- **Average DEPTH Score: 2.2**

- **Action:** Company B is on thin ice. One wrong move and they're done. Focus on treating employees fairly, especially those affected by the conflict. Publicly, silence might be golden, but they better be ready for the backlash.

Company C: Global Entertainment Company

- **Profile:** They make the stuff everyone watches, so they have a big platform and a diverse audience. They get the power of stories.

- **DEPTH Analysis:**

  - ▷ **Deliberate:** Acknowledge the conflict thoughtfully, use their reach to promote understanding, and maybe help out. **Score: 4**

▷ **Educated:** They need to understand their audience's different views and how their content might be seen. **Score: 3**

▷ **Purposeful:** Make sure their actions match their values; no exploiting the situation. **Score: 3**

▷ **Tailored:** Tell stories that build empathy; maybe team up with people directly affected. **Score: 4**

▷ **Habitual:** People will remember how they've portrayed different cultures and if they've actually cared about social issues before. **Score: 3**

▶ **Average DEPTH Score: 3.4**

▶ **Action:** Company C can do some real good here, if they are smart about it. Lift up the voices of those affected, but don't oversimplify or make it about them. Partnering with the right people can show they're serious, not just jumping on a trend.

KEY TAKEAWAYS

1. Crises reveal our flaws.

2. Clear communication is key.

3. Decisiveness, not impulsiveness, wins in a crisis.

CHAPTER 17:

LOOKING THROUGH THE DEI LENS WITH MORE DEPTH

The market likes performance, the market likes execution. As long as you're performing on what you're committed to, it's not an ESG conversation. It's not a woke conversation. It's a performance conversation."

– Haider Nazar, Co-Founder & CEO, MAIIA Global, Reputation Intelligence

Throughout this book, we've talked ad nauseam about the evolving landscape of corporate communication, and how diversity, equity, and inclusion have become indispensable pillars for any forward-thinking organization. The role of communicators is no longer confined to conveying information; it now involves creating narratives that are inclusive, equitable, and representative of the diverse employee base.

In Chapter 2, we introduced the DEI LENS. This chapter offers an expanded definition and demonstrates how a DEI LENS is a process of four steps that builds the foundation of every DEI communications strategy. The magic happens when we apply this 4-step process to The DEPTH Model.

LENS is built on the foundation that we have the responsibility to:

- ▶ **L**anguage the Promise
- ▶ **E**ngage the People
- ▶ **N**avigate the Power
- ▶ **S**trategize the Process

This foundation powers a process that helps communicators create not just compelling content, but narratives that resonate with all employees, reflect organizational values, and align with DEI goals consistently and meaningfully.

L: LANGUAGE THE PROMISE

Every organization has a brand promise and sometimes an employer brand promise or employer value proposition. Marketing teams communicate the brand promise through campaigns. HR hops on the brand wagon and communicates the employer's brand promise through the career site, how they do outreach, and the application and interview experience.

Communications gives life to the brand and employer brand promise through its language. This promise sets the tone for how employees perceive and experience the company's values, mission, and commitment to DEI. Too often, however, we sound like everyone else, and we just blend in.

Remembering what it's like for 13-year-olds, we look to belong, not stick out too much, but just be cool enough to be accepted. Much of our DEI messaging mimics this tightrope. Look at what ChatGPT provided when asked to "write a company diversity statement":

write a company diversity statement

At [Company Name], we value diversity and believe that it is essential to our success. We are committed to creating an inclusive workplace that welcomes and supports people of all backgrounds, experiences, and perspectives.

We understand that diversity encompasses more than just visible differences such as race, ethnicity, gender, sexual orientation, and age. It also includes differences in thought, culture, religion, education, socio-economic status, and abilities. We recognize that a diverse and inclusive workplace fosters creativity, innovation, and better decision-making, which ultimately benefits our employees, customers, and stakeholders.

Our commitment to diversity and inclusion is reflected in our recruitment, hiring, and promotion practices. We strive to attract a diverse pool of candidates for all positions and ensure that our hiring process is fair, equitable, and inclusive. We also provide ongoing training and development opportunities to all employees to ensure that they have the skills and knowledge to work effectively in a diverse workplace.

We believe that creating a diverse and inclusive workplace requires ongoing effort and commitment. We encourage open and honest communication, respect for different viewpoints, and the celebration of differences. We also recognize that creating a diverse and inclusive workplace is not only the right thing to do, but it also makes good business sense. It allows us to better understand and serve our diverse customer base and improves our overall performance.

At [Company Name], we are committed to promoting diversity, equity, and inclusion in all aspects of our business. We will continue to listen, learn, and take action to create a workplace where everyone feels valued, respected, and empowered to succeed.

A couple of takeaways:

1. If the ChatGPT result sounds eerily familiar because it's what your organization's statement looks like, let's break down why that is. First, we know that ChatGPT memorizes the internet, which means this is what organizations have posted on their websites at mass scale. It's just spitting back to us what is already out there.

How did we get here? Many of us need to keep doing the deep internal work to truly understand what DEI *actually* is. We thought we understood, we thought we were doing the right thing, and we did our best, but we are learning that our understanding was only surface level, as evidenced by this example, which is why we need DEPTH.

If this is hitting close to home, then make sure to go back to the section where we provide a step-by-step guide on how to put together a great DEI commitment statement in chapter 13.

2. If we can put your organization's name in the [Company Name] area and swap it with another company name in an entirely different industry, then we've slipped into the 13-year-old mentality of belonging. We buy the same clothes, have the same haircuts, listen to the same music, and like to do the same things. We lack a sense of our own individuality, our own uniqueness, and what makes us distinct that benefits the whole. Read most DEI Annual Reports and you'll see this sense of sameness.

We know how the 13-year-old story ends. Soon, they'll learn trying to blend in doesn't protect them, and they'll either have a rough time individuating, or worse, never discover who they are and continue to adopt other's identities. They could miss out on their life's purpose. Same for our organizations. It's not a great long-term strategy for our business when our success depends on exceptional stand-out talent and customer growth and we're spending our time looking like everyone else.

THE DEPTH MODEL DIFFERENTIATES YOUR ORGANIZATION

Organizations are in the midst of a major identity crisis. As society evolves, we have to keep pace and figure out who we are and what we stand for. We have demographics who fear being left behind (which ChatGPT contributes to), feel they can't keep up, or don't see themselves as a part of the future. Of course, they are going to fight for visibility, agency, and respect.

If we have unintentionally re-marginalized at any time in our DEI communications message, it's time to fix that. While we're at it, let's take the lead from our marketing and HR buddies on what makes our organization stand out to both customers and candidates and develop a strong, defensible messaging framework based on the questions posed by The DEPTH Model.

WE CONTROL THE LANGUAGE CHOICES WE MAKE

Language is the most immediate tool we have to influence the cultural identity of a workplace. When we use The DEPTH Model, we discover our identity.

For example, look at "T for Tailored." We hold strategy sessions and workshops to help companies basically "find themselves" in the DEI space. Your organization can't do all of the things, but your organization is responsible for what it can and should do. When every organization does its part, a mighty wave of change is in motion. Every organization started by identifying something in the marketplace that needed better solutions. They looked to solve a problem, a need. Let's give it life.

Language the promise by tailoring it.

1. CONSIDER: **Take** stock of capabilities.

    Ensure the message is something you can speak to from a position of strength and expertise, and help the reader see that it makes sense that you're sending this message.

    Considered question: Is this our lane?

2. CLARIFY: **Tailor** your message.

    The message can't be generic and something that can be pasted into anyone else's message. Make it clear what business you're in.

Clarified statement: We are uniquely positioned to do XYZ / we are different because LMNOP.

3. COMMUNICATE: **Tell** your story.

Expand the knowledge with what your company can uniquely do. Be specific and actionable.

Committed action: We are in the unique position to XYZ because we LMNOP.

When we dig deep into these questions with you and your leaders, we'll be able to articulate a fresh, unique, individual, valuable, and litigation-mitigating position where you won't sound like everyone else. You'll sound like you.

The 13-year-old who no longer tries to be anyone else but themselves—faults and strengths in all—is happier and feels better in their skin. The world respects and appreciates when someone exudes that level of confidence and clarity. Your organization will know what it can and cannot do, and you'll have a lot more confidence in knowing what you can and cannot message.

E: ENGAGE THE PEOPLE

Engagement is the cornerstone of successful communications, especially when it comes to DEI. Communicators must involve multiple partners and continuously gather feedback to ensure that the DEI narrative resonates across the board. With so much change afoot, we can't rely on what we've done before to still be relevant, this means we must be deliberate, the first step in The DEPTH Model.

DEI COMMUNICATIONS IS CHANGE MANAGEMENT

As an organization evolves, so will its culture. Change communications, which apply change management principles to DEI work, helps employees navigate these shifts. Communicators must clearly explain why changes are happening, how they align with the organization's DEI goals, and what employees can expect.

Like many (most?) organizational change efforts, not everyone will be on board. Some will actively resist, some will be passionate, some will wonder why it's a thing, and some will look like the Homer Simpson meme where he walks backward and disappears into the hedges. But we've been here before. We do change communications regularly in our rhythm of business. We just need to extend this experience by adding a DEI LENS.

Doing a web search and looking at The Kübler-Ross Change Curve®, the chart marks "Shock" as the first reaction that audiences will have to change, especially if they are not a part of its making. If we engage people and bring them into the change process, we'll have a higher success rate in helping folks integrate the change into their roles and daily rhythm. Here's what's really fascinating about the change curve: the same researchers also charted the grief cycle, and the experience is quite similar.

When we connect the dots and see that DEI communications need to be rooted in change management—understanding that everyone will have their own path, pace, and experience of the change, similar to the grief cycle ("Denial" → "Acceptance")—we can understand that engaging all our audiences in the creation of our messaging is essential.

We are asking people to change, and we have to be there for them as they do.

While the kind of language we use to describe the promise of our organization for every employee is important, the most effective way to come up with what to say and how to say it is to use the language employees use already. The way we find out how they think, experience, and talk about DEI as outcomes is by engaging them through engagement surveys, focus groups, employee resource groups, and by listening to dissenting voices.

Chapter 9 is devoted to leaders and engaging them in the work. Two leaders in particular can help us help the organization withstand outside pressure. Given the litigious chilling effect DEI work experiences, communicators need to stay close to HR and Legal to make sure our messaging is true and can withstand threats.

OWNING OUR NARRATIVE

There is a difference between controlling our narrative and owning our narrative. Controlling our narrative is reactive, and owning is proactive. We learn from employees how they experience DEI, from HR and Legal how we stay in compliance, and from Marketing how we are distinct. When we proactively build the messaging this way, it has a greater ability to resonate across demographics and audiences. Folks will be able to see themselves in the messaging because they were part of its creation. This also enables a smoother change curve transition.

Feedback is an essential part of engagement. We need to understand how our communications are being received by different segments of our workforce. What resonates with some might alienate others. Continuous feedback allows communicators to refine messaging, ensuring that the DEI narrative is truly inclusive and meaningful to all employees.

Engaging the people demonstrates how deliberate our messaging needs to be. Consider the questions from Deliberate to build a messaging framework that uses language that your target audiences can relate to.

Engage the people, deliberately.

1. CONSIDER: **Define** the problem.

   Contextualize the problem by finding the actionable problem in the audacious issue.

   Considered question: What are we solving for?

2. CLARIFY: **Decide** on positioning.

   Choose a position by situating the issue at the intersection of the company's core values and core capabilities.

   Clarified statement: This is what ABC company is saying . . . and why.

3. COMMUNICATE: **Do** what matters.

   Commit to action by triangulating the statement with what you can and will do to solve the problem.

   Committed action: Because ABC company believes X and is uniquely positioned to do Y, we will Z.

N: NAVIGATE THE POWER

Communicating about DEI within power structures can sometimes feel like navigating a minefield. It requires a delicate balance of transparency, authenticity, and diplomacy. In this step, communicators must assess the power dynamics at play and create a strategy that aligns with the organization's Purpose.

We don't always name the various ways power influences what we say and do. Communications as a traditional system in a business is set up to be a performative system. It rewards performative communications as business performance, as doing our job. Our leaders may affirm or disrupt that system. They feel pressure from the Board, which feels pressure from shareholders or other external pressures.

Everyone is feeling pressure to perform from everywhere. A DEI communicator can decouple performative from performance. When we ground all our DEI communications strategy work within The DEPTH Model, we're rooting it firmly in the organization's purpose. That's our strongest case, and one that leaders will respect.

Navigate the power with purpose.

1. CONSIDER: **Position** the mission.

   Make sure there is a clear connection between the situation and the purpose of the organization.

   Considered question: Is this aligned with the company's mission (and vision)?

2. CLARIFY: **Promote** the mission.

   Center the people your organization serves as part of the people impacted by the situation.

   Clarified statement: This is how the message supports our mission and advances our vision.

3. COMMUNICATE: **Publicize** the mission.

   Incorporate the mission into the message so the connection is clear.

   Committed action: Our mission to XYZ calls on us to do LMNOP.

S: STRATEGIZE THE PROCESS

The final step of the DEI LENS is about creating a sustainable, long-term strategy for DEI communications. This includes everything from the editorial calendar to partnerships, infrastructure, and metrics. To take a twist on a well-known saying, we don't rise to our goals, we fall to our processes. While we may have the best of intentions, if we're serious about implementing a powerful DEI communications strategy, we have to integrate the work from the beginning and throughout our processes.

This is where Habitual comes in handy. As we language the brand promise, engage all our target audiences, and navigate power dynamics and structures, strategizing the process allows us to build a DEI LENS onto everything we touch. It becomes who we are and how we roll.

Every piece of communication, from emails to Town Halls, should be planned with a DEI LENS. This involves reviewing your editorial calendar to ensure that DEI themes are not just reserved for special occasions or cultural observances but are part of your everyday communications. For example, using a DEI LENS in a quarterly business update might involve showcasing success stories from diverse teams or highlighting how DEI initiatives have contributed to business outcomes.

Implement your strategy into your processes like a good habit.

1. CONSIDER: **Hone** your commitment.

   Question if you are communicating to keep up with competitors, reacting to an external factor, or at a starting point where this is a pivot of greater commitment that you will sustain.

   Considered question: Is this something we have committed to before and are willing to continue?

2. CLARIFY: **Hold** the line.

   Be with impacted audiences through the good times and the bad. Show that you are not fair-weather organizations only telling positive stories during heritage months.

   Clarified statement: We've said it before, and we'll say it again.

3. COMMUNICATE: **Handle** your business.

   Culture proof points and untold stories abound in your organization. Build the infrastructure to surface them, document them, and share them to establish consistency beyond only external forcing factors.

   Committed action: What resources are needed to change our current habits?

ACTIVITIES ARE NOT OUTCOMES

Our DEI narrative needs to shift from prioritizing DEI activities to valuing DEI outcomes that lead to business outcomes. Activities are not outcomes. Communicating activities doesn't mean we're getting results; it just means we're busy doing a bunch of stuff. Many tactics, initiatives, or programs end up in the DEI Annual Report looking like a list of activities at summer camp.

Imagine a summer camp—one you might choose based on what you hope to accomplish. Whether it's science, theater, basketball, or art, the goal isn't just to partake in random activities, but to gain skills, build relationships, and grow in ways that align with your passions or goals. The same approach applies when telling the story of your company's DEI work. It's not enough to focus on the activities themselves; we need to shift our focus to the **outcomes** we are striving to achieve.

Every activity should be intentional, and outcome-driven. Focus on the **why** behind each initiative: Why are we holding a listening session? Why are we highlighting women's contributions during Women's History Month? Why are we donating to a STEM organization? The answer should always lead back to the outcomes we're aiming to achieve—psychological safety, gender equality, and economic equity, for example. We should always know how the activity is moving us closer to solving problems and meeting our DEI goals.

By shifting our DEI story from a list of activities to the outcomes that matter, we create a more compelling, impactful narrative that resonates with employees, partners, and the broader community. This shift in perspective transforms DEI from a checklist of events to a powerful tool for driving innovation, fostering collaboration, and creating lasting change in the workplace. This approach not only highlights our commitment to DEI but also ties it to the overall success and vision of the organization.

That's where the stories are; that's where we can share the vision of what the workplace could be. Here are a few examples of how common DEI activities can translate into meaningful, measurable outcomes:

Activity: Listening Sessions →
Outcome: Psychological Safety and Innovation

Listening sessions, where employees are invited to share their thoughts, concerns, and experiences, are an important activity. But the outcome we're striving for goes beyond just listening. The goal is to create psychological safety—an environment where employees feel comfortable speaking up, knowing they'll be heard without fear of retaliation or dismissal.

With psychological safety, employees are more likely to share innovative ideas and collaborate more effectively, which in turn drives business success. For example, a company that prioritizes psychological safety might see improved problem-solving, better market insights, and greater adaptability in an ever-changing business environment. Tell that story.

Activity: Women's History Month Speaker →
Outcome: Equality for Women in the Workplace

Hosting a speaker during Women's History Month can be an inspiring and educational experience, but the real outcome we're aiming for is gender equality across the organization. It's not just about hearing from an influential woman, but ensuring that all women experience equal treatment in their work environments, and that men are supported and resourced to be effective contributors as well.

The outcome of such efforts should be measurable progress in closing gender pay gaps, increased representation of women in leadership roles, and a culture where all women feel supported and empowered to succeed. Tell that story.

Activity: Donating to a STEM Organization → Outcome: Reducing the Economic Wage Gap

Many companies make donations to STEM organizations as part of their DEI efforts, but the outcome should go far beyond a one-time check. The true goal is to reduce the economic wage gap by making opportunities in STEM available to systemically underrepresented groups.

For instance, let's consider a partnership with a STEM organization that trains youth in lower socioeconomic areas to code. Donating to such a cause is important, but the outcome we're striving for is systemic change around access to opportunity and economic success. By providing ongoing support and offering internships and job opportunities to program graduates, the company helps create a lasting impact that goes beyond the initial donation. It's a relationship, not a transaction.

These outcomes aren't abstract; they're concrete, measurable improvements that demonstrate a company's genuine commitment to DEI. They show that DEI is not just about symbolic gestures but about creating meaningful change that aligns with the company's values and business goals. Tell that story.

NOT RELYING ON THE TERM "DEI" TO TELL YOUR STORY

We have the honor and opportunity as communicators to tell the greatest story ever told: DEI is a series of decisions that change policies, systems, structures, and processes and lead to outcomes that benefit and improve the lives and careers of every employee, customer, and our greater society.

We need to learn how to talk about DEI, both with and without explicitly using the term. For instance, rather than constantly repeating "DEI," we could focus on how inclusivity improves collaboration, innovation, and employee satisfaction. Say what we mean and mean what we say.

In some workplace cultures, the term itself is triggering for some demographics. Using the term in some regions and states may even be against the law. We need to be more creative anyway, and if these compelling issues are present, then let's step up.

Stepping up challenges us to truly learn what DEI is, what it can do, and the power it has to improve lives. When we better understand DEI, we tell a better story, and our audiences better understand the work. We are a part of the pivot our organizations and the greater society are looking for. We are the key.

KEY TAKEAWAYS

1. Language the promise.
2. Engage the people.
3. Navigate the power.
4. Strategize the process.

#LetsGoCommunicators

WORK WITH THE AUTHORS

Janet M. Stovall, CDE, Founder and Principal: Pragmatic Diversity

https://pragmaticdiversity.com

Mission:

Pragmatic diversity is an objective approach to the subjective "isms" that limit human and business potential. I help organizations understand the value of diversity and offer straightforward solutions to unlock that value.

Description of services:

Strategic Consulting, Keynotes, Workshops, Training Sessions, Executive Communications

Kim Clark, Founder and CEO:
Kim Clark Communications, Inc.

https://www.KimClarkCommunications.com/

Mission:

We provide strategic consultation and teach the skills needed for communicators to shift organizational communications to be meaningful, have impact, build trust with business partners, bring about a more diverse, equitable, and inclusive workplace and position organizations from a place of strength.

Description of services:

Keynotes, Workshops, Training Sessions, Strategic Consulting, Embedding DEI into the Communications Process Sessions, Inclusive Communications Guides, Inclusive Communications Content Reviews, Leader and Team Communication Assessments, and "Add Us To Your Speed Dial"-style Support, 1:1 Coaching and an On-Demand Video Course with Monthly Group Coaching.

APPENDIX

Go to TheConsciousCommunicator.com for resources, to download guides, articles, toolkits, and more.

Definitions

Accessibility: The practice of making information, activities, and/or environments sensible, meaningful, and usable for as many people as possible.

> https://www.seewritehear.com/learn/what-is-accessibility/#

Allyship: Making the commitment and effort to recognize our privilege and work in solidarity with oppressed groups in the struggle for justice. Allies understand that it is in their own interest to end all forms of oppression, even those from which they may benefit in concrete ways.

> https://www.racialequitytools.org/glossary

Accompliceship: Being willing to put our own privilege at risk in order to disrupt racism and discrimination in the workplace and beyond. It is the next step after allyship, assuming a greater degree of personal action and risk of social capital.

> https://www.diverseeducation.com/opinion/article/15106233/
> 2020-vision-the-importance-of-focusing-on-accompliceship-
> in-the-new-decade#:~:text=Accompliceship%20means%20
> being%20willing%20to,in%20the%20workplace%20and%20
> beyond.

Advocacy: Covers a range of strategies and tactics designed to move people to action. The tools of advocacy include: messaging, research and data, power analyses, education, personal influence and persuasion, coalition building, organizing, and action.

> https://www.racialequitytools.org/resources/act/strategies/
> advocacy

Belonging: Being seen for our unique contributions, feeling connected to our coworkers, being supported in our daily work and career development, and being proud of our organization's values and purpose. It is created by multiple people, as opposed to "fitting in," which places the responsibility for entering a group solely on the person entering.

> https://hbr.org/2021/06/what-does-it-take-to-build-a-culture-
> of-belonging

CDO/CDIO: Chief Diversity Officer/Chief Diversity and Inclusion Officer. The highest-ranking executive tasked with accountability for compliance, advocacy, and education of the company related to diversity, equity, and inclusion. The CDO serves as a resource for leadership and employees and is a representative of the community.

https://www.forbes.com/sites/mariaminor/2021/05/03/
heres-the-bottom-line-reason-why-companies-need-a-chief-
diversity-officer/?sh=6600b85a7bc3

Communicators: A professional content creator who speaks on behalf of organizations, messaging internally and externally through leaders or channels, regardless of "communications" being formally in their title.

Content Creators: Responsible for the ideation and creation of content that connects a brand or entity to its prospective audience. Content creation encapsulates copywriting, design, production, and other media that provide value and connect you to your target audience.

https://www.siegemedia.com/creation/content-
creator#:~:text=A%20content%20creator%20is%20
responsible,you%20to%20your%20target%20audience.

Cultural Appreciation: When someone seeks to understand and learn about another culture in an effort to broaden their perspective. Gives visible credit, pays members from the culture for their talent.

Cultural Appropriation: Taking one aspect of a culture that is not our own and using it for our own personal interest or gain.

DEI Communications Skills: A learned skill that takes practice. It can be fraught with mistakes that, when acknowledged, examined, and taken seriously, can inform new and next choices. These capabilities allow us to proactively identify exclusion in our work, processes, teams, and strategies. Mastering them enables communicators to align organizational DEI strategy and communications, and establishes communications as a critical factor in implementing DEI organizationwide.

DEI Communications Role: Designated role within an organization dedicated to finding DEI message gaps and opportunities. Often tasked with teaching DEI communication skills to others, this role does not have to be solely responsible for reviewing and approving all DEI content. The role can be internal and full-time, reporting to the Chief Diversity Officer or fulfilled by an external consultant. Ideally, this role is embedded in every line of business across the organization, similar to HR and finance.

DEI Communications Lens: Focusing on opportunities to be more inclusive and representative in communications. Actions include:

- ▸ Thinking and acting beyond oneself and one's own experiences;
- ▸ Learning from others who are different;
- ▸ Including everyone's needs and experiences in the development of work and decisions;
- ▸ Designing work and processes for the most marginalized groups to benefit all marginalized groups.

Diversity: All the ways in which people differ, and characteristics that make one individual or group different from another. It is all-inclusive, recognizes everyone and every group, and values difference.

https://www.racialequitytools.org/glossary

Employee Resource Group (ERG): A voluntary, employee-led diversity and inclusion initiative that is formally supported by an organization. ERGs generally are organized on the basis of common identities, interests, or backgrounds, with the goal of supporting employees by providing opportunities to network and create a more inclusive workplace. Organizations design different types of resource groups such as ERGs, business resource groups, belonging resource groups, affinity groups, inclusion resource groups, or network groups.

https://www.gartner.com/en/human-resources/glossary/
employee-resource-group-erg-

Equity: Fairness and justice; not the same as equality. Whereas equality means providing the same to all, equity means recognizing that we do not all start from the same place and must acknowledge and make adjustments to imbalances. The process is ongoing, requiring us to identify and overcome intentional and unintentional barriers arising from bias or systemic structures.

https://www.naceweb.org/about-us/equity-definition/

Inclusion: Intentionally bringing traditionally excluded individuals and/or groups into processes, activities, and decision-/policy-making in a way that shares power.

https://www.racialequitytools.org/glossary

Inclusive Language: Inclusive language acknowledges diversity, conveys respect to all people, is sensitive to differences, and promotes equal opportunities.

https://www.linguisticsociety.org/resource/
guidelines-inclusive-language

Intention: A state of being which involves our alignment, motivation, and processes. It is not simply a goal at which you arrive; intent arrives before we do.

https://deborahljohnson.org/

Intersectionality: Professor Kimberlé Crenshaw coined the term in 1989 to describe how race, class, gender, and other individual characteristics "intersect" with one another and overlap.

Lived Experience: Personal knowledge about the world gained through direct, first-hand involvement in everyday events, rather than through representations constructed by other people.

https://www.oxfordreference.com/view/10.1093/oi/authority.20110803100109997

Majority Coding: The more marginalized one's position is in society, the more aware they are of the nuances of power and privilege, which are most often culturally coded. The dominant culture is reinforced by language used to keep the status quo, which ends up being exclusionary by default.

https://deborahljohnson.org/

Social Justice: A communal effort dedicated to creating and sustaining a fair and equitable society in which each person and all groups are valued and affirmed.

https://www.ccsu.edu/johnlewisinstitute/terminology.html

Microaggressions: Everyday verbal, nonverbal, and environmental slights, snubs, or insults, whether intentional or unintentional, which communicate hostile, derogatory, or negative messages to target persons based solely upon their marginalized group membership.

https://www.racialequitytools.org/glossary

Performative Action: Efforts that are unintentional, unsupportable, and unaligned with stated beliefs. Positive intent that has little or no impact on the dismantling of systemic inequity.

Transformative Communications: The opposite of performative communications. Authentic dialogue that actually moves the needle positively on a given issue. Transformative communications requires selective consideration, entering a social dialogue, rather than just initiating a corporate monologue, and communicating with depth. Transformative communications brings the power, might, and potential of the business world into the service of changing things. Transformative communications is what The DEPTH Model seeks to operationalize.

Unconscious Bias: Mental shortcuts that lead to snap judgments—often based on race and gender—about people's talents or character, that impact our decisions, language, and treatment of others.

https://hbr.org/2021/09/unconscious-bias-training-that-works

Virtue Signaling: The act of speaking or behaving in a way that's meant to demonstrate one's good moral values. For example, proclaiming support for an issue on social media to imply true concern. Generally associated with disingenuousness and lack of meaningful impact, and primarily motivated by the desire to signal one's good moral values, regardless of whether it leads to a meaningful outcome.

https://effectiviology.com/virtue-signaling/

Visual Inclusion: Graphics, images, illustrations, video, and photography that are intentionally inclusive by design; designed with visual representation from the conceptual or ideation stage.

Visual Representation: Is mainly the direct or symbolic reflection of something in the format of photos, images, memes, and graphics to represent people, things, a place, or a situation.

https://www.igi-global.com/dictionary/visual-representation/69112#:~:text=Visual%20representation%20is%20mainly%20the,a%20place%2C%20or%20a%20situation

ACKNOWLEDGMENTS

JANET

A book is a moment in time. But if you're lucky, a lifetime of loving hands and forgiving spirits bring you to that moment. I'm so damn lucky.

Thank you, Kim Clark, for saying, "Let's write a book"—and meaning it. Thank you for doing all the work—and I mean all—to keep it on track and out front. Good friends don't let you do stupid sh*t ... alone. Thank you for being the heart in our work. Thank you for being both co-author and friend.

Thank you, Maia and Alexis, for feeding, forcing, and forgiving me in whatever measure was needed. For being my biggest cheerleaders and most honest critics. For being my creative muses and mechanics. For twerking for the Cicero, and all the other awards. For growing into the kinds of women I am always so, so proud of and so, so motivated to make proud of me (ya'll know I'm ugly crying right now, right?). I love you more than you can ever know.

Thank you Mama, for bringing me into this world and for shaping me into someone who could move through it with strength, sass, and sophistication. Thank you Daddy, for never accepting anything less from me than the best I could do (and then pushing for just a little better). I wish you were here to touch this book, but know that your hands guided every word. Thank you, Vallin SFAS, for believing that me writing a book was both no big deal and a very big deal, and for asking about that ISBN number so you could check the catalog at your store. Thank you, Alicia, for taking such good care of my mama—and me—so I could do what I needed to do to do this. Thank you family for shaping, supporting, and spurring me. Being a Stovall is the greatest inspiration and aspiration of my life.

Thank you brilliant, beautiful, Black women in my life—sisters, soulmates, and support who were with me long before and all the way through this work and everything leading up to it. Terri, for being my friend since we were girls together. Judy, for always trying (and mostly succeeding) to keep me out of trouble. Smiley, for being and making me beautiful. Alexis and Dara, for knowing when my solitude needed interrupting. Valeria W., for bringing me into this space and keeping me in it. Valeria L., for reminding me that everything is working for my highest good (and for being the living proof of that). My NLI queens— Camille, Shade, Michaela, Shelby and Yvonne—for feeding my spirit with your brains, beauty, and boldness. Karen B., for being the kind of mom that made me feel okay about being the kind of moms we are. Hilda—to whom I'm granting honorary sister status—for teaching the girls all the wonderful bad habits they need, and for always being there (even when you didn't know you were).

Thank you, Davidson family, for being part of my becoming and staying part of my being; for loving me in spite of myself; for being both the good friends who would bail me out of jail and the best friends who would be right there in the cell with me, saying "Damn, that was fun!"

Thank you RMSH family for being with me in the beginning and sticking with me to the end.

Thank you, Steve and Cathy, for being the best neighbors anyone could ever have. You have no idea what having you next door has made possible.

Thank you, Dean, for convincing me to do a TED talk; for asking me the three questions backstage that got me onstage and the one question, "What does trouble look like for you?," that drives me to dare. Thank you, Lisa, James, Brian, Sammy and Austin, for being the best damn communications team I have ever worked with. Thank you, Jon and Mason, for building and bolstering my video runway to the world. Thank you to all the UPSers and NLIers who have and continue to believe in me.

Thank you, MikeD (mikedshotme.com), Shade (fcolasimbo.com), Shelby (shelbywilburn.com), Smiley (smileyshairclinic.com), and Nyssa (thegreenroomagency.com), for shooting, steering, and styling me for those bomb-ass single photos.

KIM

I love that there's a standard section in books where we get to celebrate gratitude! No one does anything important alone and I'm grateful for my incredible support system giving me the creative freedom, the intellectual challenge, the spiritual tools, the physical and emotional sustenance to just be and be my best, however that's showing up right now.

Thank you first to Janet M. Stovall. You took this kid from California seriously when we first met at a tapas restaurant and said yes to co-authoring this book at a time when you had many options and opportunities. You made the right choice. :) People needed to hear from you on this and you brought skills to the table that elevated this work to something I couldn't have imagined. Thank you for your "yes." It's an honor to partner with you, teach with you, learn from you, and be your friend. I'll get as many cousins as I can for as long as I live.

Thank you to my mentor and teacher, Rev. Dr. Deborah L. Johnson, of whom I've been a student since 2004. You are ahead of your time and also right on time, for a time such as this. I have you to thank for leading me towards this career, teaching me about my deepest intent, and being the best teacher anyone could ask for. You pushed me to speak on bigger stages and encouraged me. Your belief in me never waivers. Your work and legacy will forever be enshrined by the work of those who listen and act on your wisdom and guidance. Thank you for your gracious giving in all that you have for the good of all.

Thank you to my family, my friends, my girlfriend, and my kids. Your support and air cover made this all happen. Jordan and Kaiyan, you are my heart, my heroes, my motivation. I tell you this all the time, but I'll say it again and again: I love you! To Kristy, thank you for your incredible patience, support, love, healthy food, laughs, and most especially, your beautiful heart. I'm so fortunate that lightning crashes. To my mom, there are not enough words to demonstrate how your advice, presence, and unconditional love have led me to be the woman I'm becoming. Thank you, Dad, for your relentless cheerleading no matter what endeavor I find myself doing. Thank you to my sister, for her help with writing social content and getting my butt in gear to write more and share what I learned to help more people. Shout out to our sister, who passed in 1985. I know you are here and one of my guardian angels. To my grandmother Iola, for her quiet strength, wisdom, and giving me a Native American name that I so cherish, that I wear shoes of the same name: gazelle. To my grandfather Don, who showed me early and often that I can design my own destiny and to follow what I love. To my grandmother Ellen, thank you for all the dirty jokes that remind me to have fun and treasure life.

To Dr. Kimb Massey, thank you for being my critical thinking professor (so much of this work is your fault) and thesis faculty advisor back in the day and being a constant foundation for me as I grow personally and professionally. I am so grateful for our friendship and our late in-the-night conversations about life.

Thank you to Chelsea Delaney, who not only contributed an article, but also stepped in to help me get over my overwhelm of a blank page and a head full of ideas. Your coaching, notes, reviews, encouragement, and skills in making some of my verbose interviews turn into succinct points are a true gift.

Thank you to my business coaches, for sharing your hits and misses to help me learn.

Thank you to the Internal Communications Support Group, that showed up for each other every Friday for a year. You proved to me the value of community within our discipline and across global borders. You inspired me. You helped me write portions of this book in my head and have always been a great support for this work. Some of you have even changed your roles and careers to focus on DEI Communications and I am so excited to see the impact you will have in changing the communications discipline and industry by applying a DEI LENS on all of your work. You've got this.

Thank you to my partner firms, who gave me support, grace, and space to write: Ragan Consulting Group and Employera. I am lucky to have such a great crew to work with.

AUTHORS' ACKNOWLEDGEMENTS

The authors collectively want to thank Publish Your Purpose, specifically Jenn, Bailly, and Lisa. Thank you for recognizing the value of our idea immediately and taking a chance on first-time book authors. Your support system for authors and assembling a great team of editors—especially Nancy, who made our book flow. And thank you to Amita Mehta for the initial introduction.

We are so grateful to Anthony Foxx for your contribution to the Foreword. Your willingness to contribute some of your thought leadership to support this work means the world to us. Thank you.

Thank you to each person who said yes to providing testimonials: Celeste Headlee, Sally Kohn, Jennifer Brown, Anita Ford Saunders, Loral Langemeier, David Lee, Nicole "Nikki" Clifton, April Thomas, LaQuenta Jacobs, Jim Ylisela, Andy Getsy, Lauren Antonoff, Irana Wasti, Kirsten Goodnough, Gael Adams-Burton, Imma Folch-Lázaro, Elizabeth Bunney, Martha Hanlon.

Thank you to each Deeper Dive contributor for your time, your expertise, and willingness to participate in the book. We learned from you and appreciate the work you're doing in the world. You are each heavy-hitters and to have you all contributing together in this book just takes it to a whole new level. You helped us role model what it looks like to co-create work. Rev. Deborah L. Johnson, Shirley Anne Off, Kimberly Massey, Ph.D., Vikki Conwell, Chelsea Delaney, Miriam Khalifa, David Murray, Charlene Thomas, Dr. Jennifer A. Richeson, Lily Zheng.

Thank you to Austin Josey, for the graphics in the book, video editing for our YouTube channel, and for The Conscious Communicator brand. You signed on early and immediately and we are so grateful!

Thank you to our legal, operations, finance, marketing, and PR teams, who believe in the importance of the work and helped us with their gifts to raise the awareness that we all can be the change we want to see in the world.

Thank you to Luci Valentine Photography based in San Francisco, CA, for the cover photo and finding us the coolest couch in the city for the photoshoot. Thank you to Larisa Roberts, for keeping us on time and finding a stain remover quickly. Thank you to Diana Anaya for hair and makeup. Thank you to Katie Quinn and Jessica Holland for the wardrobe ideas. Thank you to Leslie Gomez for getting our heads on straight. Thank you to Fani Nicheva and Bob von Elgg for the book cover design. Book cover design is a lot harder than some may think.

Ultimately, we must thank all the conscious communicators around the world. You've been through so much and yet here we are at a time of significant change where your organizations need you to lead. You are talented, important, valued, and essential to the health and wellbeing of your employees and external constituents. What you do every day matters. Thank you for taking this consciousness and multiplying it. Thank you for doing the hard work to make the right decisions. Thank you for signing on to "do no harm." You are the present and future of how communications will be done. You are changing the industry and your legacy will have a long lasting impact. We have you to thank. Thank you.

WORKS CITED/NOTES

1963 Stanford Research Institute Internal Memo, cited in Freeman RE, Reed DL. *Stockholders and Stakeholders: A New Perspective on Corporate Governance.* California Management Review. 1983;25(3):88–106.

"2022 Edelman Trust Barometer." Edelman. https://www.edelman. com/sites/g/files/aatuss191/files/2022-01/2022%20 Edelman%20Trust%20Barometer%20FINAL_Jan25.pdf.

"A New Era of Workplace Inclusion: Moving from Retrofit to Redesign." Future Forum. Accessed March 11, 2021. https:// futureforum.com/2021/03/11/dismantling-the-office-moving-from-retrofit-to-redesign/.

Abdow, M. "Media Consumption is Over the Top: How Much and Where to Spend is Key to Maximizing ROI." Forbes. n.d. Retrieved from: https://www.forbes.com/sites/forbesagency council/2021/04/08/media-consumption-is-over-the-top-how-

much-and-where-to-spend-is-key-to-maximizing-roi/
?sh=237770c72bd9.

"Alternative facts." Wikipedia. Accessed July 2, 2022. https://en.wiki-pedia.org/wiki/Alternative_facts#:~:text=%22Alternative%20 facts%22%20was%20a%20phrase,President%20of%20the%20 United%20States.

"Associated Press Stylebook." www.apstylebook.com. Accessed June 21, 2022. https://www.apstylebook.com/blog_posts/18.

"APA Dictionary of Psychology." American Psychological Association. Accessed March 21, 2022. https://dictionary.apa.org/.

"Aunt Jemima Rebrands as Pearl Milling Company." Pepsico. com. Accessed February 7, 2022. https://www.pepsico.com/ news/press-release/aunt-jemima-rebrands-as-pearl-milling-company02092021.

Austin, J. L., & Urmson, J. O. How to do things with words: The William James lectures delivered at Harvard University in 1955. Harvard Univ. Press. 2009.

"Availability Bias." Catalog of Bias. n.d. https://catalogofbias.org/ biases/availability-bias/.

Bender, E. M., Gebru, T., McMillan-Major, A., & Shmitchell, S. (2021). On the Dangers of Stochastic Parrots: Can Language Models Be Too Big? Proceedings of the 2021 ACM Conference on Fairness, Accountability, and Transparency, 610–623.

Blakeslee, Sarah. "The CRAAP Test," LOEX Quarterly: Vol. 31: No. 3, Article 4. https://commons.emich.edu/loexquarterly/vol31/ iss3/4.

Blodgett, S. L., Green, L., & Schneider, B. (2020). Demographic dialectal variation in social media: A case study of African American English. Language Variation and Change, 32(2), 185–215.

Brady, W. J., Crockett, M. J., & Van Bavel, J. J. (2022). The MAD model of moral contagion: How moral emotions spread through networks. Trends in Cognitive Sciences, 26(1), 68–78.

Burgess, Wade. "A Bad Reputation Costs a Company at Least 10% More Per Hire." Harvard Business Review. https://hbr.org/2016/03/a-bad-reputation-costs-company-at-least-10-more-per-hire#:~:text=The%20top%20three%20factors%20associated.

Bursztynsky, J. (2023, June 15). Meredith Whittaker believes AI is 'replicating patterns of inequality. Fast Company. https://www.fastcompany.com/90908974/why-meredith-whittaker-believes-ai-is-replicating-patterns-of-inequality.

"Business Roundtable Redefines the Purpose of a Corporation to Promote 'an Economy That Serves All Americans.'" Businessroundtable.org. August 19, 2019.https://www.businessroundtable.org/business-roundtable-redefines-the-purpose-of-a-corporation-to-promote-an-economy-that-serves-all-americans.

Carucci, Ron, and Praslova, Ludmila N. "Employees Are Sick of Being Asked to Make Moral Compromises." Harvard Business Review. Accessed February 21, 2022. https://hbr.org/2022/02/employees-are-sick-of-being-asked-to-make-moral-compromises%20?utm_medium=social&utm_source=instagram&utm_campaign=have2haveit.

Charlton, James I. Nothing About Us Without Us: Disability Oppression and Empowerment. University of California Press, 2000.

Cikara, M., Bruneau, E. G., & Saxe, R. (2020). Their pain gives us pleasure: How intergroup dynamics shape empathic failures and counter-empathic responses. *Journal of Personality and Social Psychology,* 118(6), 1135–1163.

"Combating Anti-Asian Hate." Accessed June 21, 2022. https://www. aapihatecrimes.org.

"Conscious & Unconscious Biases in Health Care: Two types of bias." Georgetown University National Center for Cultural Competence. Accessed July 4, 2022. https://nccc.georgetown.edu/bias/ module-3/1.php.

Cramer, M. "Maker of Eskimo Pie ice cream will retire 'inappropriate' name." The New York Times. Accessed February 7, 2022. https:// www.nytimes.com/2020/06/20/business/dreyers-eskimo-pie-name-change.html.

"Delivering what matters: Equitable vaccine access globally." Retrieved from https://about.ups.com/us/en/social-impact/the-ups-foundation/health-humanitarian-relief/delivering-what-matters--equitable-vaccine-access-globally.html.

Deuze, M. "McQuail's Media & Mass Communication Theory." Los Angeles: Sage, 2020.

"Diversity and Inclusion." www.adobe.com. n.d. https://www.adobe. com/diversity.html.

"Diversity & Inclusion—Careers." n.d. www.bostonscientific.com. https://www.bostonscientific.com/en-US/careers/working-here/diversity-and-inclusion.html.

Dumenco, Simon. "More Than 950 Brands Participated In 'blackout Tuesday' On Instagram, Plus The Latest Jobs Numbers In Context: Datacenter Weekly." AdAge. n.d. https://adage.com/article/

datacenter/more-950-brands-participated-blackout-tuesday-ins-tagram-plus-latest-jobs-numbers-context-datacenter/2260916.

Edelman Report: Cycle of Distrust Threatens Action on Global Challenges. n.d. World Economic Forum. Accessed June 21, 2022. https://www.weforum.org/agenda/2022/01/edelman-trust-barometer-2022-report/.

"EEOC Releases Fiscal Year 2020 Enforcement and Litigation Data | U.S. Equal Employment Opportunity Commission." www.eeoc.gov. Accessed February 26, 2021. https://www.eeoc.gov/newsroom/eeoc-releases-fiscal-year-2020-enforcement-and-litigation-data.

Ely, Robin and Thomas, David A. *Getting Serious About Diversity: Enough Already with the Business Case.* Harvard Business Review 98, no. 6 (November–December 2020).

Evan, W., & Freeman, R. E. In T. Beauchamp, & N. Bowie (Eds.), *Ethical Theory and Practice* (pp. 75–84). Englewoods Cliffs, N.J.: Prentice Hall. 1993.

"Fact finding in the information-age." n.d. Retrieved July 2, 2022. https://www.crf-usa.org/images/pdf/fact_finding.pdf.

"Factsheet on Persons with Disabilities." The United Nations. Accessed January 11, 2022. https://www.un.org/development/desa/disabilities/resources/factsheet-on-persons-with-disabilities.html.

Fiske, S. T., Cikara, M., & Cuddy, A. J. (2017). Why ordinary people torture enemy prisoners. *Proceedings of the National Academy of Sciences,* 113(20), 5492–5497.

Franklin, Chris. "Tweet Message." *Twitter,* May 31, 2020, https://twitter.com/campster/status/1267183124582215680?lang=en.

Freeman, Edward. "Stakeholder Theory—Edward Freeman." Stakehold-ermap.com. 2010. https://www.stakeholdermap.com/stakeholder-theory-freeman.html.

Frothingham, Scott. "How Long Does It Take for a New Behavior to Become Automatic?" Healthline. Healthline Media. October 24, 2019. https://www.healthline.com/health/how-long-does-it-take-to-form-a-habit.

Graves, Stephen R. "Are You a Tone-Deaf Leader?" Dr. Stephen R. Graves. n.d. https://stephenrgraves.com/articles/read/dont-be-a-tone-deaf-leader/.

Greenwald, Anthony G., and Mahzarin R. Banaji. "Implicit social cognition: attitudes, self-esteem, and stereotypes." Psychological Review 102.1 (1995): 4.

"Guidelines for Inclusive Language | Linguistic Society of America." www.linguisticsociety.org. n.d. https://www.linguisticsociety.org/resource/guidelines-inclusive-language.

"Hamlet, Act I, Scene 3, Open Source Shakespeare." Accessed April 24, 2022. https://bit.ly/37zqiGp.

Hanlon, Martha. n.d. https://www.wideawakebusiness.com.

Harjo, Joy. Crazy Brave: A Memoir. W. W. Norton & Company, 2012.

Haynes, J.D. "Unconscious decisions in the brain." Max-Planck-Gesellschaft. Accessed February 10, 2022. https://www.mpg.de/research/unconscious-decisions-in-the-brain.

"Henry Schein Cares Foundation Launches Third Phase of 'Wearing Is Caring' Campaign Public Health Awareness Campaign to Promote Health Equity Regarding COVID-19 Vaccines." Accessed February 5, 2022. https://investor.henryschein.com/

news-releases/news-release-details/henry-schein-cares-foundation-launches-third-phase-wearing.

Higginbotham, G., Zheng, Z., Yalda, T. (2021). *Beyond Checking a Box: A Lack of Authentically Inclusive Representation Has Costs at the Box Office*. Los Angeles: Center for Scholars and Storytellers, UCLA.

"How Black Twitter and Other Social Media Communities Interact with Mainstream News." Knightfoundation.org. Accessed June 21, 2022. https://knightfoundation.org/features/twittermedia.

"How to measure the cost of a bad reputation." Alva Group. Accessed December 12, 2021. https://www.alva-group.com/blog/how-to-measure-the-cost-of-a-bad-reputation/.

Jenkin, Matthew. "Ice-Cream Icon Jerry Greenfield Shares His Top Tips for Business Startups." The Guardian. n.d. https://www.theguardian.com/small-business-network/2013/jun/21/ben-and-jerrys-business-startups-tips.

Jones, C. "For faces behind Aunt Jemima, Uncle Ben's and cream of wheat, life transcended stereotype." USA Today. Accessed May 9, 2022. https://www.usatoday.com/story/money/2020/07/10/real-people-behind-aunt-jemima-uncle-ben-cream-of-wheat/3285054001.

Kahneman, D. *Thinking, fast and slow*. Penguin, 2012.

Kellerman, Barbara. "When Should a Leader Apologize-and When Not?" Harvard Business Review. n.d. https://hbr.org/2006/04/when-should-a-leader-apologize-and-when-not.

Kendi, I. X. *How to be an antiracist*. One World, 2019.

Kennedy, V. "Does corporate diversity and inclusion enable systemic racism?" Medium. Accessed December 31, 2021. https://medium.

com/@kennedyesq516/does-corporate-diversity-and-inclusion-enable-systemic-racism-ab329b9749ba.

Kern-Foxworth, M. *Aunt Jemima, Uncle Ben, and Rastus: Blacks in Advertising, Yesterday, Today, and Tomorrow*. Greenwood Press, 1994.

"Korn Ferry | Organizational Consulting." www.kornferry.com. Accessed June 21, 2022. https://infokf.kornferry.com/rs/494-VUC-482/images/The%20invisible%20power%20of%20the%20reference%20man.pdf.

Krentz, Matt. 2019. "Survey: What Diversity and Inclusion Policies Do Employees Actually Want?" Harvard Business Review. February 5, 2019. https://hbr.org/2019/02/survey-what-diversity-and-inclusion-policies-do-employees-actually-want.

Leading the Social Enterprise: Reinvent with a Human Focus: 2019 Deloitte Global Human Capital Trends. Deloitte. 2019. https://www2.deloitte.com/content/dam/insights/us/articles/5136_HC-Trends-2019/DI_HC-Trends-2019.pdf.

Maine, D. A. "Andy Murray politely reminds reporter of the existence of Venus and Serena Williams." ESPN. Accessed June 8, 2022. https://www.espn.com/espnw/culture/the-buzz/story/_/id/17307649/andy-murray-politely-reminds-reporter-existence-venus-serena-williams.

"Mavs Take Action!" The Official Home of the Dallas Mavericks. n.d. https://www.mavs.com/mavstakeaction/.

McEvoy, J. "Mrs. Butterworth's to Undergo a 'Complete Brand and Packaging Review' Along with Aunt Jemima, Uncle Ben's." Forbes. Accessed May 9, 2022. https://www.forbes.com/sites/jemimamcevoy/2020/06/17/mrs-butterworths-to-undergo-a-complete-brand-and-packaging-review-along-with-aunt-jemima-uncle-bens.

Meissner, C. A., Wang, C., & Wheatley, T. (2023). The neuroscience of implicit bias. *Annual Review of Psychology*, 74, 401–427.

Mishel, L., & Kandra, J. "CEO pay has skyrocketed 1,322% since 1978: CEOs were paid 351 times as much as a typical worker in 2020." Economic Policy Institute. Accessed March 19, 2022. https://www.epi.org/publication/ceo-pay-in-2020.

Moise, I., DiNapoli, J., & Kerber, R. "Exclusive: Wells Fargo CEO ruffles feathers with comments about diverse talent." Reuters. Accessed July 4, 2020. https://www.reuters.com/article/us-global-race-wells-fargo-exclusive/exclusive-wells-fargo-ceo-ruffles-feathers-with-comments-about-diverse-talent-idUSKCN26D2IU.

"National estimates for News Analysts, Reporters, and Journalists." Retrieved from U.S. Bureau of Labor Statistics: https://www.bls.gov/oes/current/oes273023.htm.

O'Neil, C. (2016). Weapons of math destruction: How big data increases inequality and threatens democracy. Crown.

"Our Commitment—Business Roundtable." 2019. Business Roundtable. 2019. https://opportunity.businessroundtable.org/ourcommitment/.

"Political Action Committees." Open Secrets.: Accessed June 4, 2022. https://www.opensecrets.org/political-action-committees-pacs/2022.

"Polo Ralph Lauren Introduces New Collection That Builds Upon Its Historic Partnership With Morehouse and Spelman Colleges." Businesswire. Accessed June 8, 2022. https://investor.ralphlauren.com/news-releases/news-release-details/polo-ralph-lauren-introduces-new-collection-builds-upon-its.

Powell, John A. www.news.berkeley.edu/2021/01/25/to-end-white-supremacy-attack-racist-policy-not-people/. Accessed June 29, 2022.

"Reflecting Society: The State of Diverse Representation in Media and Entertainment." World Economic Forum. n.d.

"Reverend Deborah L. Johnson." Deborah L. Johnson. Accessed June 21, 2022. https://deborahljohnson.org.

Rhenman, Eric. "Industrial democracy and industrial management. A critical essay on the possible meanings and implications of industrial democracy." 1968.

Secretary, H. H. S. O. of the, & Assistant Secretary for Public Affairs (ASPA). "Fact Sheet: Explaining Operation Warp Speed." HHS. gov. Accessed February 6, 2022. https://web.archive.org/web/20201219231756/https://www.hhs.gov/coronavirus/explaining-operation-warp-speed/index.html.

Section 508 of the Rehabilitation Act in the U.S. https://www.ada.gov/508/#:~:text=Overview,and%20members%20of%20the%20public.

Sinek, Simon. *Transcript of 'How Great Leaders Inspire Action.'* www.ted.com. 2009. https://www.ted.com/talks/simon_sinek_how_great_leaders_inspire_action/transcript?language=en.

Sinek, Simon. n.d. https://simonsinek.com.

Steigrad, A. "Ad Spending Expected to Hit New Highs Post-COVID." Retrieved from New York Post: https://nypost.com/2021/06/14/ad-spending-expected-to-hit-new-highs-post-covid.

"Targeted Universalism | Othering & Belonging Institute." Belonging.berkeley.edu. n.d. https://belonging.berkeley.edu/targeted-universalism.

"The Costly Business of Discrimination." The Center for American Progress. n.d. www.americanprogress.org/article/the-costly-business-of-discrimination.

"The Curb-Cut Effect (SSIR)." Ssir.org. Accessed April 26, 2020. https://ssir.org/articles/entry/the_curb_cut_effect.

"The Power of Habit." The Washington Center for Cognitive Therapy. Accessed June 21, 2022. https://washingtoncenterforcognitivetherapy.com/the-power-of-habit/#:~:text=Once%20a%20behavior%20becomes%20automatic.

Thompson, J. D. *Organizations in action: Social science bases of administrative theory*. McGraw-Hill, 1967.

"Understanding the DEI Backlash." www.linkedin.com. Accessed June 21, 2022. https://www.linkedin.com/pulse/understanding-dei-backlash-kim-clark/.

"UPS Calls For Justice And Reform To Advance Equality." Retrieved from https://about.ups.com/us/en/newsroom/press-releases/diversity-equity-inclusion/ups-calls-for-justice-and-reform-to-advance-equality.html.

"UPS Supports Equitable Distribution of COVID-19 Vaccines Worldwide." Retrieved from https://about.ups.com/us/en/social-impact/the-ups-foundation/health-humanitarian-relief/ups-supports-equitable-distribution-of-covid-19-vaccines-worldwi.html.

Vaid-Menon, Alok. *Beyond the Gender Binary*. Penguin Workshop, 2020.

Valinsky, Jordan. "Eskimo pie is getting rid of its derogatory name." ABC7 Chicago. Accessed May 9, 2022. https://abc7chicago.com/eskimo-pie-new-name-edys-products-brands-that-have-changed-offensive-names-with-racist/6945191/#:~:text=Eskimo%20

Pie%20has%20decided%20on,the%20company's%20 founders%2C%20Joseph%20Edy.

Wallace, A. "Uncle Ben's has a new name: Ben's original." CNN. Accessed February 7, 2022. https://www.cnn.com/2020/09/23/ business/uncle-bens-rice-rebrand-bens-original/index.html.

"Wells Fargo CEO apologizes for remark about diverse talent." Reuters. Accessed July 4, 2022. https://www.reuters.com/article/global- race-wells-fargo/wells-fargo-ceo-apologizes-for-remark-about-di- verse-talent-idUSL3N2GK37W.

Wertheim, Suzanne Ph.D. Accessed May 27, 2022. https:// www.linkedin.com/posts/suzanne-wertheim-ph-d-1508464_ inclusivelanguage-ukraine-activity-6903119740781387776- La-7/?inf_contact_key=5987b9980a8560f853f1e- c3a9f49e522&utm_medium=member_desktop_web&utm_ source=linkedin_share.

Wikipedia. (n.d.). 2022 Buffalo shooting. https://en.wikipedia.org/ wiki/2022_Buffalo_shooting

Wu, K. J. "Land O'Lakes drops the iconic logo of an Indigenous woman from its branding." Smithsonian.com. Accessed February 7, 2022. https://www.smithsonianmag.com/smart-news/ mia-land-olakes-iconic-Indigenous-woman-departs-packag- ing-mixed-reactions-180974760/.

Zeitchik, S. (2013, February 8). *For David O. Russell, An Entry in His Own 'Silver Linings Playbook.'* Retrieved from Los Angeles Times: https://www.latimes.com/entertainment/movies/la-xpm-2013- feb-08-la-et-mn-for-david-o-russell-a-real-life-silver-linings-play- book-20130208-story.html.